The Covent Garden Guide

By Douglas Gardner
With 47 Illustrations and Street Map

Ernest Benn Limited, London
In association with Edward Stanford
Limited, Covent Garden

First Edition 1980

Published by Ernest Benn Limited
25 New Street Square, London EC4A 3JA
& Sovereign Way, Tonbridge, Kent TN9 1RW

©Ernest Benn Limited 1980
Printed in Great Britain
by W & J Mackay Limited, Chatham
Typeset by Cold Composition Ltd.,
Tonbridge, Kent
ISBN *Paperback* 0 510 01635-9

Contents

Introduction	page 7
Approaches to Covent Garden	9
Covent Garden Today	11
The Square and The Market	17
St Paul's Church	27
Bow Street and the Fieldings	37
Theatre Royal Drury Lane	45
The Royal Opera House	59
Transport Museum and Theatre Museum	69
The Streets of Covent Garden	73
Shopping in Covent Garden	103
Guide to Shops and Services	106
Theatres, Restaurants and Hotels	115
Index of Streets and Landmarks	118
Street Map	121
Acknowledgements	127

Introduction

The aim of this guide is to help and encourage visitors to enjoy Covent Garden in its entirety, its buildings, thoroughfares and byways, its richly-peopled history, its individuality, and everything it has to offer in its new surge of vitality and creativity.

Vitality and creativity. These words, in fact, sum up the importance and fascination of Covent Garden today and throughout the seven centuries of its existence. Art, literature and music have all flourished in the area together with the great theatrical tradition that began in Drury Lane and carried Covent Garden's Royal Opera House to its present pinnacle of international fame.

The old fruit and vegetable market once provided a colourful background to Covent Garden life. This has gone, but an element of the market tradition persists in and around the fine buildings that housed it; and many of the enterprises have clear links with the crafts of the past.

But why Covent Garden? The almost universal answer is that it is an unexplained corruption of Convent Garden, springing from the fact that there was once at this place a convent garden, owned by the Abbey of Westminster; but the dictionary shows that covent was the original word from which convent was derived (the Anglo-French version of the French *couvent*). It is not surprising that this earlier word was retained, or re-enlisted, since it is so much easier on the tongue than Convent Garden. Given the alternative, the forbears of Shaw's Eliza Doolittle would be in no doubt as to which should be used on the way to market at four or five o'clock in the morning.

The attractiveness of Covent Garden has much to do with its position near to but effectively separated from the centre of London, and with the appeal of its overall design, a splendid inheritance from Inigo Jones. The area flourished early on as a meeting place, its coffee houses and taverns acting as a magnet for everyone connected legitimately or otherwise with literature, art and drama—all this going on side by side with night life of the seamiest sort and every category of crime.

Law is in better order now, thanks to the Runners of Bow Street and their successors, and Covent Garden is still a good meeting place, thanks to its excellent restaurants, pubs and cafes. And with many new attractions such as the Transport Museum and the imminent Theatre Museum it is one of the pleasantest places in London in which to spend a few hours.

The Covent Garden Guide is divided into two main sections. The first, beginning on page 17 and ending on page 71 contains more information—chiefly about Covent Garden's fascinating history—than could be read comfortably whilst walking about. This section should be read in an armchair beforehand if possible, or else during a break at an early stage of the exploration.

From page 73 onward the information is about specific streets and features, and it is provided in as compact a form as possible so that it will serve the needs of the visitor when afoot in Covent Garden. The arrangement there is a logical one designed to enable the visitor to deal with the streets, theatres and other points of interest in one area at a time. However, the information relating to a particular point can be traced quickly by referring to the Street Index and noting the page number of the street that is wanted.

Covent Garden is a place for walking. It can be crossed from end to end or from top to bottom in about ten minutes, and yet within its boundaries there are enough little streets to keep one meandering almost endlessly according to inclination. A single form of map reference is used for all the lists of streets, landmarks, theatres, shops and so on, so that each can be found in the map square referred to—and it may be useful to know that you can walk across one square of the grid in about one minute.

Approaches to Covent Garden

The traffic management scheme is still under discussion at the time of going to press, but the intention is to keep all through traffic out of Covent Garden, especially the inner areas, and some parts are to be confined to pedestrians.

By Car. The surrounding roads for through traffic are The Strand, Aldwych, Kingsway, High Holborn, Monmouth Street, St Martin's Lane and Charing Cross Road. Routes designated for local distribution are Endell Street, Long Acre, Garrick Street, Bedford Street and Chandos Place on the west side, and Great Queen Street, Wild Street, Kemble Street, Russell Street and Wellington Street on the east side.

Car parks on the west side can be reached from Upper St. Martin's Lane and Bedfordbury. On the east side parking for 400 cars is available under the New London Theatre off Drury Lane (open 24 hours).

Underground. Covent Garden station on the Piccadilly Line gives immediate access to the heart of Covent Garden, but at the time of going to press this station is closed on Sundays. Near alternatives are Leicester Square (Piccadilly Line and Northern Line), Holborn (Piccadilly Line and Central Line), Tottenham Court Road (Northern Line and Central Line), and Charing Cross (Northern, Bakerloo and Jubilee Lines).

By bus. The Aldwych bus stop is served by the following numbers: 1, 1A, 4, 6, 9, 9A, 11, 13, 15, 55, 68, 77, 77A, 77C, 170, 171, 172, 176, 188, 239, 501, 502 and 513. Charing Cross Road is served by numbers 1, 24, 29 and 176. High Holborn is served by numbers 19, 22 and 38.

British Rail. Charing Cross station, a terminal for many lines from the south and south-east, gives access to Covent Garden via the Strand.

Covent Garden Today

In the Covent Garden of today there is an echo of its distant origins. The opportunity that Inigo Jones detected, and brilliantly exploited, in the perfectly situated convent garden acres was reflected in the 1970's by the opportunity that arose when the fresh produce market moved out and left something like a square mile close to the centre of London open for redevelopment.

This time, however, it was an opportunity that very nearly slipped away. The initial response of London's planners was to consider using it for extending the West End, removing most of the existing historic buildings and erecting in their place new hotels, conference centres and bright-light tourist attractions. These ideas met with fierce opposition. Covent Garden, it was discovered, had an army of admirers, people who loved it not only for the architecture of Inigo Jones and William Fowler but also for its individuality, the interest and friendliness of the maze of streets that surround the square in strangely complementary contrast, and for the many haphazard details that give the area character and atmosphere.

These people forcibly expressed their views and then helped the GLC to write a new plan which was given the title of the Greater London Council (Covent Garden) Action Area Plan. This ten-year project has been put into operation with the backing of the various groups in the area. Some, however, question the likelihood of all the good intentions being translated into action, and community activists continue to be involved with the GLC in monitoring the progress of the plan.

An area of 90 acres has been designated for conservation, the main market buildings have been retained and rehabilitated, and it is intended to encourage the setting up of a wide variety of specialist shops, crafts and small businesses, together with an appropriate number of restaurants, wine bars, exhibition centres and similar enterprises geared to relaxation. Some trading restrictions are also visualised to preserve the village atmosphere.

Covent Garden's traditional role in the theatrical field is also expected to be encouraged. There is no place for massage parlours, strip clubs, casinos and gambling clubs but some limited scope is provided for night clubs, discotheques and restaurants with music and dancing. Public houses are also safeguarded.

The fine lines of the old market building, now in use as a modern shopping centre.

One of the slightly chilling phrases used by the planners, 'pedestrian circulation', does in fact point to new or regained pleasures for those who walk around in Covent Garden. The new pedestrian square for the Piazza recaptures the original concept of Inigo Jones under the inspiration of the squares he had admired in Italy, and pedestrian routes with a network of small spaces and gardens linked to them are among future good intentions.

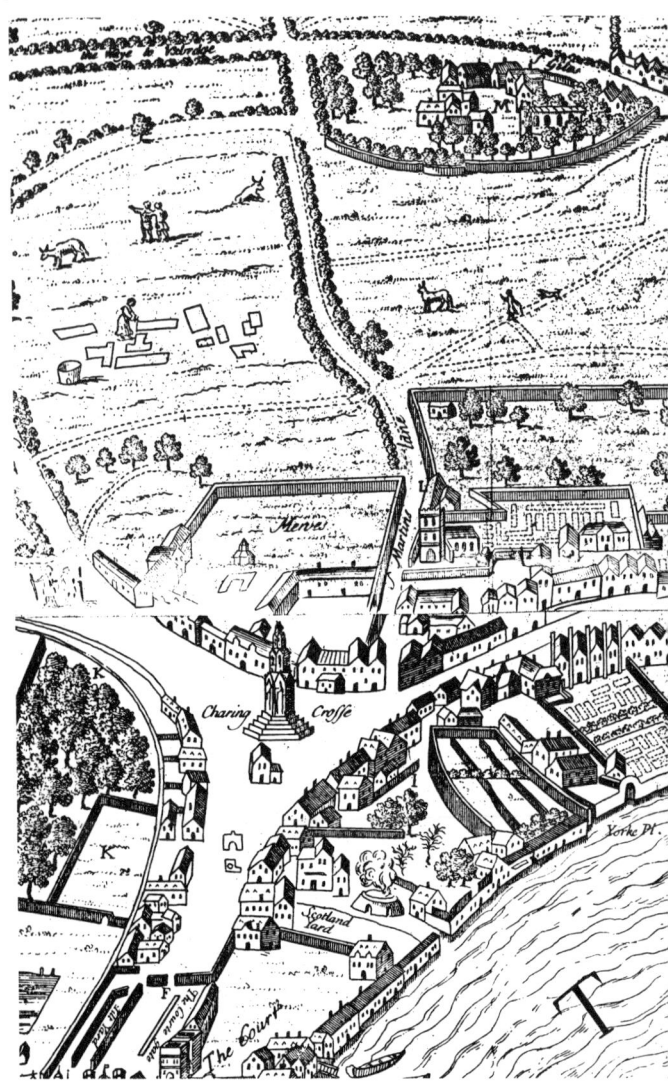

The rectangular field with trees and small buildings in this map of 1560 by Ralph Aggas is the convent garden, tended by the monks of Westminster, from which Covent Garden arose. The extraordinary development that took place in the ensuing 160 years can be seen by comparing this map with the Sutton Nicholls engraving on the next two pages showing the Piazza in c 1717-28.

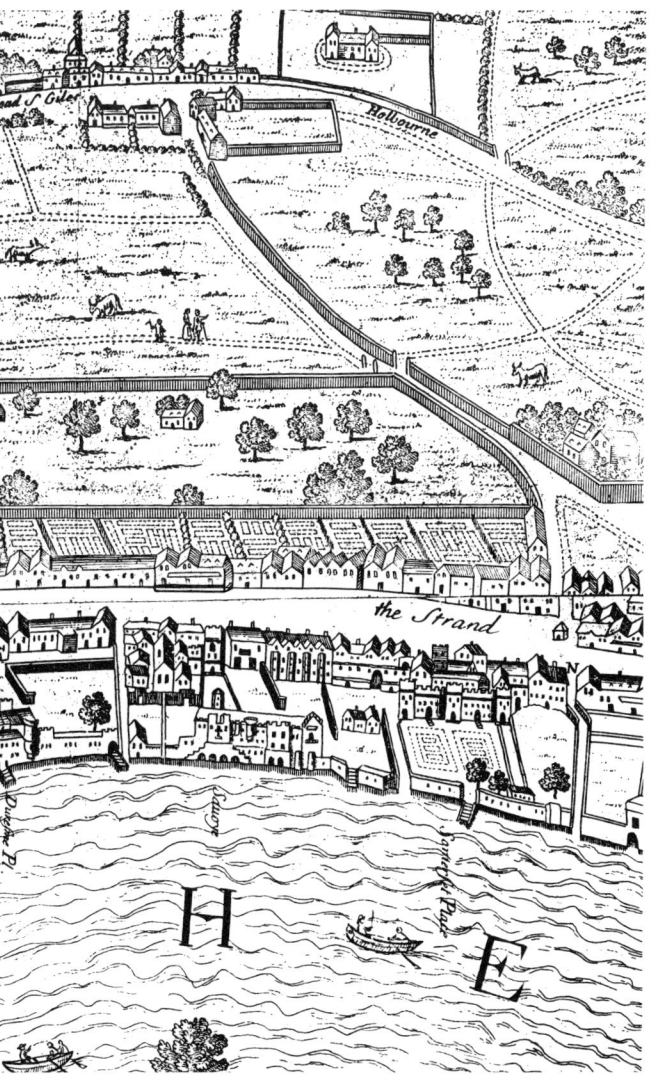

The Square and The Market

The great square is the heart of Covent Garden. With its Piazzas, St Paul's Church, and the distinctive market buildings that are just beginning a new life, it is also the natural starting point for an exploration of Covent Garden of today and yesterday.

The Central Market Building, splendidly restored with its appealing Victorian design intact, has been given a new role as a leisure and entertainment area with a complex of shopping arcades, street cafés, galleries and small workshops. The Flower Market, listed among buildings of special architectural or historic interest, with its remarkable cast iron arcades, now has a fascinating future as the home of the Transport Museum and Theatre Museum. But these buildings also serve as a permanent monument to the tradition of buying and selling fruit and vegetables—and, later, flowers—that has only recently come to an end after flourishing more or less continuously since at least the twelfth century. And by tracing the source of this tradition we come to the origin of Covent Garden itself.

The ancient convent garden tended by the monks of Westminster was enclosed within a stretch of land owned by the abbey foundation between the abbey and the city of London. There is a reference to a garden of the Abbot of Westminster in a document as early as about 1200, and early maps show a cultivated pasture with trees, enclosed by a wall, where Covent Garden now exists.

The monks grew apples, pears, plums, medlars and nuts, as well as vegetables, in this very fertile patch of reddish brick earth. It was ideal for growing crops of this kind as it warmed up quickly in the spring.

Whatever they did not need for themselves the monks sold on the spot to augment the income of the foundation. And it was this latter part of the operation that clearly sowed the seeds of the future great market, for their activities created an incentive for others to bring their own produce. Many changes came, but through them all and through the centuries the market persisted and flourished, even though it was never a market in the strictly legal sense until a charter was granted for it by Charles II in 1670.

With the Dissolution of the Monasteries Westminster's convent garden became the property of the crown. Edward VI gave it to the Duke of Somerset, but when he fell from favour—far enough to be beheaded—it reverted to the crown; and in 1552 it was granted to

John Russell, Earl of Bedford, together with 'seven acres, called Long Acre'. And over the ensuing years it was the Russells who were mainly instrumental in the creation of Covent Garden.

They began by building a town house, known as Bedford House. It was relatively simple at first but was later rebuilt and developed. Its frontage faced the Strand, and at the back there were eventually stables, a formal garden and a terraced walk protected by a wall that in due course became the south wall of the square.

For a while the Russell gardeners and some others maintained the local production of fruit and vegetables. Supplies were also brought in by people living in nearby villages, which helped to keep pace with the ever-growing demand from the swelling population of London; and these supplies took over completely when the remaining cultivated land in Covent Garden gave way to the great building scheme.

Recollections of other early buildings close to Bedford House survive in local street names. Burleigh House, owned by Lord Burleigh, stood where Burleigh Street now runs; and Exeter Street is a further reminder of the same house, which was renamed Exeter House when his son, Sir Thomas Cecil, became Earl of Exeter. And in a lane running off the Strand a lovely house was built by Sir William Drury, giving its name to Drury Lane.

Many small houses also arose early on, especially along the north side of the Strand, and it would have been logical to predict a haphazard development from then on within the natural guidelines of the Strand, Drury Lane, Long Acre and St. Martin's Lane. However, a number of circumstances combined to bring into existence for Covent Garden a positive and unified concept—one that was never totally realised but which nevertheless produced a magnificent result.

This happened early in the seventeenth century, and a key factor was the recent blossoming in England of a taste for good architecture, which included especially an appreciation of the buildings travellers were seeing in Italy. Charles I, who came to the throne in 1625, was one of those Englishmen with good taste in architecture and he took early steps to improve the quality of building in London. He set up a Commission for Buildings, with powers to enforce standards and limit development, and one of its executives was Inigo Jones.

Inigo Jones was almost certainly the most accomplished and knowledgeable architect of his time. What is more he had lived for many years in St. Martin's Lane, was a justice of the peace for Westminster, and was intimately concerned with Covent Garden.

In the 18th century the square was used for recreation as well as buying and selling produce from the country. Popular activities including football, cricket, boxing and wrestling. Dogs had their own ideas.

The final and most operative circumstance affecting the transformation of the area was the desire of the fourth Earl of Bedford to develop his Covent Garden property, prompted by the need to restore the financial situation of the family and an awareness of the demand for housing on the outskirts of rapidly growing London.

All these strands came together when the earl asked Inigo Jones to produce a plan for Covent Garden. He rose to the occasion brilliantly with a bold scheme for a square surrounded by arcades on the model of the piazza at Livorno and other Italian towns.

The involvement of the influential architect, and the obvious excellence of his scheme must have helped in overcoming the formidable difficulty in the way of obtaining permission to build. Nevertheless the Earl of Bedford had to pay £2000 for a licence, and the dispensation included instructions by the king himself that the new buildings must provide a 'distinguished ornament' rather than a mere extension to London.

In fact the extraction of that £2000 probably ensured that the finished product was a little less ornamental than it might have been. A contemporary, with space-age foresight, lamented the missed opportunity to give London 'one of the finest squares in the universe'.

A compromise had to be reached, and instead of providing arcades on all four sides of the square, as originally planned, Inigo Jones had to settle for two arcades, with the garden wall of Bedford House remaining on one side and the church occupying the centre of the fourth.

Even so, Londoners were completely carried away by the magnificence and originality of the square as it took shape and flocked to watch its development. This was around the year 1631, more than thirty years before the plague and the Great Fire of 1666, and the new square was in unbelievable contrast to the closely packed tenements of the city at that time.

With its spacious Italian atmosphere, the whole square was originally referred to as the Piazza, but eventually this term remained attached only to the arcades, the northern arcade becoming known as the Great Piazza and the eastern one as the Little Piazza. All the houses in the scheme were built in magnificent style. Those incorporating the arcades were designed with the upper floors projecting above them to give a flush front elevation.

With all this splendour the earl achieved his objective. The square became one of the most fashionable parts of London, the houses being taken by titled or distinguished people including the Duke of Richmond, the Earl of Oxford, the Marquis of Winchester, the Earl of Sussex and the Bishop of Durham. Sir Peter Lely had a house which was occupied by Sir Godfrey Kneller and subsequently Sir James Thornhill.

Eventually many coffee houses and taverns sprung up in and around the square—Will's, Button's and Tom's among the more famous of them. The Bedford Coffee-house, a notable resort of critics in the time of Garrick and Quin, was under the Piazza in the north-east corner.

St Paul's Church was one of the happiest features of Inigo Jones's Covent Garden scheme and, skilfully rebuilt after a fire, it looks into the square on the west side today virtually as it did at the beginning. Nothing better has emerged in the way of a description than the promise made by the architect when the financially hard-pressed earl instructed him, 'I would not have it much better than a barn'. 'Well, then,' Jones replied, 'you shall have the handsomest barn in England.' St. Paul's has a section to itself further on (see p. 27.).'

When the square was finished the streets leading to it began to take shape. They took appropriate names, the most obvious being King Street and Russell Street. James Street was named after the Duke of York, subsequently James II, and Henrietta Street after Henrietta Maria, King Charles's queen. Nearby Bow Street derived its name simply enough from its bow shape.

The parish of St Paul, Covent Garden, came into being in a roundabout way as the new buildings grew up. The earl needed to find a way of frustrating the vicar of St. Martin in the Fields, who claimed that the new church should be under his wing as a chapel of ease because it was in his parish. The outcome was a special Act of Parliament creating the new parish of Covent Garden, which accorded the earl the right of patronage for St. Paul's Church.

All this time the market people continued with their trading. They set up stalls by the wall of Bedford House and served increasingly as an outlet for the produce of a new race of people who grew fruit, vegetables and flowers solely for sale—the first market gardeners.

And the growth of the market continued during the Civil War—possibly even more readily because of the temporary

An early view of the north-west façade of the Charter Market built by William Fowler in 1829-30 and rehabilitated in 1980.

absence of the fifth earl, William Russell, who went off to serve the deposed King Charles. The Parliamentarians took over Bedford House and sold its furniture and tapestries to swell their funds. The gold and silver plate escaped them as it had been sent for safe keeping to Woburn and Chiswick.

Private enterprise robberies were also more frequent at this time from the houses of other absent followers of the King, and records indicate that a gibbet somewhere in Covent Garden did something to discourage the habit.

The fifth earl eventually changed sides and wisely concentrated on administering his estates. His attentions included paying half the cost of erecting a column, surmounted by a sundial, in the centre of the square. It appears in many illustrations of the period and stood until 1790. He saw that the market could be a useful source of income and asked King Charles for a Royal Charter. In 1670 this was granted. Eight years later he made an arrangement with Adam Piggott and Thomas Day, giving them the right to run the market on payment to the earl of £80 a year. The agreement included measures to prevent unsightly building and to keep the area clean, and it continued in operation until 1699.

Other markets around London, including Spitalfields, handled fruit and vegetables, but none seriously rivalled Covent Garden, which slowly took over more and more of the square with a growing shambles of unsightly booths and sheds. Miscellaneous traders, including vendors of illicit gin, added to the chaos. All this, together with the mounting congestion of traffic in the square and surrounding streets, drove out the wealthy residents. Their magnificent houses were taken over by market people and the underworld, and many of them soon became totally derelict.

The decline was arrested at last by Acts of Parliament early in the nineteenth century. The booths and sheds were swept away and the covered market was built for the duke by William Fowler. He gave the building Tuscan columns, a triangular pediment and arcades to blend with St Paul's and the surviving piazzas.

Respectability thus belatedly returned, and Covent Garden Market became, through the Victorian and Edwardian years and into recent times, a much-loved institution, a place of lively activity, colourful sights and language, robust humour and a universal friendliness that took in without discrimination workers, sightseers, ballerinas, down-and-outs, top-hatted Moss Bros. customers and anyone else who found themselves threading their way among the boxes, baskets and barrows of this remarkable world.

Early morning porters and herb sellers take over as the night revelry wanes. An 1876 photograph by J. Thompson.

St Paul's Church

In the original grand design for Covent Garden, St. Paul's church was to be its focal climax; and this intention was not in the least frustrated by the earl's request that it should be 'not much better than a barn'. In the event, the promise of Inigo Jones that it should be the handsomest barn in England was more than adequately fulfilled. His design for the church combined simplicity with beautiful proportions and great dignity; and whilst blending with the square as a whole it was clearly the most important feature and so acted as a positive focal point. This we can still see, because the exterior has retained more or less its original appearance in spite of, or with the aid of, careful renovation.

Work was begun on the church, the first new Anglican church since the Reformation, in 1631. It was completed in 1633 and consecrated in 1638, the delay being due to the dispute over the question of patronage between the earl and the vicar of St. Martin in the fields.

Another problem arose over the siting of the altar. The Bishop, William Laud, was adamant that it should be against the east wall, and the result was that the great entrance from the Tuscan portico facing the square could never be used. Small side doors had to be used instead.

The ground plan of the building is a double square 100ft × 50ft, the height is 35ft, and the portico projects a further 23ft. The original workmanship was not all that it should have been, and in 1727 about £400 was spent on restoring the portico. In 1788 a major renovation was undertaken by Thomas Hardwick, including the replacement of the original plaster with Portland stone and the reconstruction of the flanking gateways in stone.

A few years later, in 1795, there was a disastrous fire which destroyed all except the walls, the portico and the south-west wing. It seems to have been started by the carelessness of plumbers who were doing some work there, and a contemporary account speaks of 'an immense pyramid of flame rising thrice the height of the building' and of the heat being felt to the end of Russell Street. Lost in the blaze were the ceiling painted by Edward Pierce, a Lely portrait of Charles I and 'the valuable and celebrated organ'.

Hardwick again took charge of the restoration and, as before,

The fire which destroyed the interior of St Paul's Church on September 17, 1795 with 'an immense pyramid of flame'.

resisted calls for modification made by people who were unable to appreciate the beauty of the original simplicity. He reproduced the original Inigo Jones concept faithfully. The present organ was originally built in 1861 by Henry Bevington and may have incorporated parts of the earlier organ by William Gray. Restoration work was carried out on it in 1967 by N. P. Mander.

There was a slight departure from the original design in 1871. It was carried out by William Butterfield, who constructed a raised chancel and bricked up the east doors. The east windows (1968-9) are by Brian Thomas.

St. Paul's has always been closely involved in the life of Covent Garden. At the time of the plague its rector, Simon Patrick, instead of following those who fled for safety to the country, stayed behind to look after the stricken and the dying and officiate at the mass funerals. His only anxiety, the records indicate, was over the possibly 'prejudicial effects' of the autumn winds when he was burying the dead at night.

A more compelling complaint on another subject was made by the under-sexton of St. Paul's in a letter to the *Spectator* on March 16, 1711. He wrote with natural pride of his practically unbroken record of tolling the bell for prayers over a span of twenty years, and then goes on to say: 'which Office I have performed to my great satisfaction, till this Fortnight last past, during which Time I find my Congregation take the Warning of my Bell, Morning and Evening, to go to a Puppet-Show set forth by one *Powell* under the *Piazzas*. By this Means I have not only lost my two Customers, whom I used to place for Six-pence a-piece over against Mrs *Rachel Eye-bright,* but Mrs *Rachel* her self is gone thither also.'

We are forced to admire the opportunist puppeteer as much as we sympathise with the under-sexton who, trusting impiously in the power of the Press, asked the *Spectator* to 'lay this before all the

World, that I may not be made such a Tool for the future.'

The loyalty of the congregation has apparently varied greatly through the years, the many counter-attractions available in the square possibly helping to cultivate the habit of choosiness among Covent Garden's inhabitants. John Wesley, predictably, did not fail to attract a good audience when he spoke at St. Paul's on November 28, 1784. He wrote in his journal: 'it is the largest and best-constructed parish church that I have preached in for several years, yet some hundreds were obliged to go away, not being able to get in.'

Many years earlier, in 1700, a full attendance drawn by a popular speaker ended in tragedy. A gallery collapsed under the strain and, as a broadsheet of the time records: 'There was nothing but Confusion for a Considerable time, some crying out Help, some Murther, and some Fire. The Dr. being forc't to leave his Pulpit, being peirc't to the heart with the Outcrys and Groans of his Auditory whose Confusion was ye may be sure very Astonishing . . . . . . among the several People who were look't upon as Dead and taken up for so, it pleas'd God but four were found really Dead. One was niece to the Man at the Black-boy in Bedford Street.' A less flourishing period is dealt with by an anonymous poet in the following terms:

Oh! how it puts me on the rack,
To see a *pedant* cloath'd in black,
Mumble a *sermon* to himself,
To save his lungs and get the pelf;
While all around, the simple sheep
Fatigu'd with grazing—fall asleep.

St. Paul's is known as the actors' church. Many famous people of the theatre are buried there and commemorated by memorials.

Left: The East Prospect of St Paul's Church.
Below: The West Prospect of Covent Garden as 'invented by Inigo Jones, 1640'.

Inigo Jones, the architect of Covent Garden.

But the church has strong connections with all the arts, reflecting the richness of Covent Garden life in general, and it is the resting place of more celebrated people than anywhere else in London apart from Westminster Abbey and St. Paul's Cathedral.

The burial ground was closed in 1853 and turned into a memorial garden paved with its tombstones—whose inscriptions have now been trampled into oblivion or nearly so. The many memorial panels on the walls inside the church have a better prospect of survival.

One of the first to be buried in the church was Robert Carr, Earl of Somerset, who once lived in Russell Street but owes his place in St. Paul's to the fact that his only daughter married its creator, the Earl of Bedford. This was the last but not the only advantage he enjoyed through patronage, for he was pardoned and set free after being found guilty of murdering his friend, Sir Thomas Overbury, the poet. Both were in love with the beautiful Countess of Essex. She preferred Carr and, because of him, sought an annulment of her reluctant marriage to young Essex; and when the poet, Sir Thomas, tried to stop this she found a way of getting him confined to the Tower, where he died mysteriously in agony. Soon after her marriage to Carr they were tried for the murder and found guilty, together with two accomplices. The latter were promptly hanged, Carr was pardoned and his wife was freed two years later. The end of the story is more rewarding. They were shunned by society and lived unhappily ever after.

There was a particularly splendid funeral at St. Paul's in 1670. The central character, who arrived via Tyburn and a lying-in-state at the Tangier Tavern in St. Giles's, was the French highwayman Claude Duval. He was a popular romantic hero, bedecked with a reputation for gallantry to feminine victims and for dancing even in his riding boots better than the best masters in London; and at his funeral there was a long trail of grief-stricken mourners. Some say that he was buried under the central aisle of the church and removed later, others that his body is still there, and still others that it never was. All agree that he was captured at Mother Maberley's tavern in Chandos Street, The-Hole-in-the-Wall.

Nobody questions the presence of Samuel Butler—to the left of the west front. Not the one who wrote *Erewhon* but the author of the anti-Puritan mock-epic *Hudibras,* which was embraced at the time as the wittiest satire in the English language, though not by Pepys who 'tried by twice or three times reading to bring myself to think it witty'.

To appreciate Pepy's problem, and admire his doggedness, we can savour such lines from *Hudibras* as:

> He'd run in debt by Disputation,
> And pay by Ratiocination,
> All this by Syllogism true
> In Mood and Figure, he would do.

Butler died in his lodgings in Rose Street in 1680, apparently penniless though not in debt. There were not more than about twenty at his funeral, but one of them was Aubrey, the diarist.

The year 1680 also saw the burial in St. Paul's of Sir Peter Lely, who had lived in the north arcade since 1662 and whose sitters had included Charles I, Nell Gwynne, Cromwell and many beauties at the court of Charles II. He was joined in 1717 by Pierre Tempest, admired for his *Cries of London,* and in 1827 by Thomas Rowlandson, whose gorgeous caricatures captured alive his entire age and much of every other.

Although, properly enough, St Paul's Cathedral finally claimed him, J. M. W. Turner began life in Covent Garden and was baptized in its church in 1775. His parents had a barber's shop in Maiden Lane when he was born, and they were married in St Paul's church.

The celebrated wood carver, Grinling Gibbons was buried in St Paul's church in 1721, and Thomas Arne in 1778. A monument to Arne on the north wall includes the first line of his setting of *Rule Britannia, the Ode in Honour of Great Britain,* which forms the finale of his patriotic masque, *Alfred.* He wrote the music for nearly ninety stage productions.

W. S. Gilbert was baptised in the church on January 11, 1837, and went on from there, through his partnership with Arthur Sullivan, to become one of the most popular of all contributors to the repertoire of the stage.

Another dexterous user of words, but without the end-product of popularity, was a predecessor, John Wolcot, who was buried in St. Paul's in 1819. He was, in fact, the best hated man of his day by virtue of the odes he propelled from his lodgings in Covent Garden under the pen-name of Peter Pindar. Victims of his lampooning lash included Sir Joseph Banks, Pitt, George III—a little more gently—and that 'tomtit twittering on an eagle's back', James Boswell. But Wolcot was not a totally consistent destroyer. He appreciated the artistic talents of the young Cornishman, Opie, encouraged him and brought him to London and eventual success.

Among the theatrical people buried in the actor's church are William Wycherley, Ellen Terry (her ashes are kept in the south wall), and Charles Macklin, whose memorial incorporates a graphic reminder that he killed a fellow actor in a green room quarrel at Drury Lane over a wig, thrusting at him with a stick which pierced his eye.

Memorial panels around the walls carry the names of actors and actresses and other stage people, right up to modern times, who have made distinctive contributions to theatrical tradition. And the church houses the offices of the Actors' Church Union and The Religious Drama Society of Great Britain. Actors read the lessons at many services.

Looking at the deep and sheltering eastern portico of St. Paul's church we can see that it is a natural gathering place—perhaps, even, a place that invites dramatic expression as does an empty stage. This has sometimes been confirmed by events. Before the electoral law changes of 1872 the portico was the hustings, or 'platform', for the Westminster elections, which were extremely robust operations. During the two or three weeks that they lasted the candidates and their friends scrambled daily for voters, dispensing food and drink and sometimes offering all kinds of other inducements. Supporters vilified the opposing candidates with broadsheets, chanting and jingles, and quite frequently the rivalry developed into physical battles. Among those who have been central figures at the Covent Garden hustings were Sir Cecil Wray, Fox (who had a majority of only 235 over Wray in a crucial election in 1784), Hood and Sheridan.

In the eighteenth century the portico was a magnet for night and early morning revellers and all who served them or hung around them. Hogarth shows Tom King's Coffee House right in front of it, a very unprepossessing hut, with a collection of people from all walks of life inside and out. Tom King served all comers with refreshment and in spite of the obvious space limitations also ran the place as a brothel. It was described as a port of call for 'the eminent, the eccentric and the notorious'. After his death his wife, Moll King, carried on the colourful tradition until she was overtaken first by a legal conviction and then, apparently, by a religious one, being last heard of as a regular Hampstead churchgoer. And the Coffee House was swept away.

The portico of St. Paul's also presided over the birth of that remarkable character Punch, descendant of a long line of English clowns, and there is now a commemoration of this event every year

This print of a Westminster election—probably in 1784—includes Fox, the Prince of Wales and the Duchess of Devonshire. It was a winning day for Fox, and also, apparently, for the pickpocket.

in the form of a puppeteers' service and May Fayre. An inscription on the wall of the church also refers to the occasion. Punch was the star of what was, in fact, a highly sophisticated and elaborate miniature theatre, set up in a booth and fitted with all the equipment, wings, backcloths and other attributes of full-scale theatres of the period. It even had footlights when they were apparently still unknown in most major theatres. Martin Powell, the disrespecful genius who used the church bell as the warning bell for his own performances, is said to have made a miniature replica of the machinery which Inigo Jones had created for operating the scenery and flying effects of court masques in the previous century. Powell's theatre, and others like it, contributed significantly to theatrical history. They experimented with new forms, including documentary presentations foreshadowing the newsreel, and political satire using marionettes and live actors. Melodrama was in full swing in the miniature theatres more than half a century before it had the tears flowing in the royal theatres.

All these things actually happened; but for many people the event in the portico of St Paul's that is most vividly remembered is the stage—and screen—meeting between Shaw's Eliza Doolittle and Professor Higgins. A snatch of conversion from the opening pages of *Pygmalion* will help to recreate the scene:

The flower girl: Let him mind his own business and leave a poor girl—
The note taker: Woman: cease this detestable boohooing instantly; or else seek the shelter of some other place of worship.
The flower girl: I've a right to be here if I like, same as you.
The note taker: A woman who utters such depressing and disgusting sounds has no right to be anywhere—no right to live. Remember that you are a human being with a soul and the divine gift of articulate speech: that your native language is the language of Shakespear and Milton and The Bible; and don't sit there crooning like a bilious pigeon.
The flower girl: Ah-ah-ah-ow-ow-oo!

And later, when she has scrambled into a taxi and asked to be driven to 'Bucknam Pellis—where the King lives.'

Taximan: What business have you at Bucknam Pellis?
Liza: Of course I hav'nt none. But I was'nt going to let him know that. You drive me home.
Taximan: And where's home?
Liza: Angel Court, Drury Lane, next Meiklejohn's oil shop.
Taximan: That sounds more like it, Judy.

Punch and Judy, still full of life, first saw the light of day in the shelter of St Paul's Church. The event is now celebrated each year with a puppeteers' service and May Fayre.

Bow Street and the Fieldings

Bow Street is famed far beyond the immediate confines of Covent Garden as the birthplace of the British police force. And it deserves the fame in spite of the fact that the event is remembered so well mainly because the first small band of crime fighters established there acquired the romantic name of the Bow Street Runners.

We are closer to the heart of the matter, however, if we also bear in mind that they were referred to at the outset as 'Mr Fielding's People'. For it was Henry Fielding who—after becoming a magistrate in 1747 to supplement the inadequate income of a successful novelist—set in motion the machinery for halting and reversing the plague of rogues, thieves, and murderers who were ravaging the entire country. Sadly, he was able to savour little or nothing of success in this battle during the many gruelling years in which he waged it—together with his blind half-brother, John, who eventually succeeded him. The Fieldings saw clearly what was needed but the masterly plans they put forward were never seriously considered until the final days of John's administration.

But there was another achievement that was not delayed, and which was possibly even more important. For the Fieldings of Bow Street established a style of justice—utterly against the existing trend—in which fairness and compassion were paramount. It is a style now taken for granted, but the Fieldings created it.

The area in which the Fieldings administered justice was in fact a part of the realm where the counter-attack against crime was probably more urgently needed than anywhere else. Through the years the splendid houses of Covent Garden had gathered around them the smaller habitations of the people who served them, and after that the crowded tenements of a subsidiary wave of satellites. The whole area became riddled with dark alleys and caves where crime and corruption seethed, and where anyone who walked unguarded could only do so in high expectation of being set upon and robbed.

When Henry Fielding observed this scene, and wrote about it so vividly, the kind of protection offered to the public was scarcely better than it had been in Shakespeare's time, depending on a

Events of this kind were sufficiently familiar in the 18th century to find a natural place as a scene in the old comedy Humour of Covent Garden.

But for the heroic intervention of the Bow Street Runners, vividly depicted here in a contemporary print, history might have been radically changed through the massacre of the entire Cabinet of George IV whilst they were dining with the Earl of Harrowby on February 23rd 1820. The conspirators, led by Arthur Thistlewood, a former lieutenant in the Lincoln Militia, were taken by surprise whilst assembling for the dark deed at 8 o'clock that day in Cato

The Hay-loft Plot of Thistlewood and his 24 Cons

Street, Edgware Road; and the print records the moment when Bow Street Police Officer Smithers, stabbed by cool and articulate Thistlewood, falls into the arms of Police Officer Sermon. The documentation of the drama is complete, down to the contents of boxes in the room. The conspirators in this 'Hay-loft plot' were said to number 24, and there were never more than 12 Runners at any time.

system whereby citizens were enlisted for service as constables, much as juries are called up today. But the duty could be delegated, and it usually ended in the hands of ancient and rheumatic 'Charlies' who could do little more than keep themselves upright with the staves that were officially intended for upholding the law. There was still a completely topical ring about the encounter that Shakespeare portrayed in *Much Ado About Nothing:*

Dogberry: This is your charge: you shall comprehend all vagrom men; you are to bid any man stand, in the Prince's name.

Second Watch: How if 'a will not stand?

Dogberry: Why, then, take no note of him, but let him go; and presently call the rest of the watch together, and thank God you are rid of a nave.

Fielding, Hogarth and John Gay were among those who were profoundly aware of the misery as well as the lawlessness around them. Gay's amusing but penetrating *The Beggar's Opera*, set in the slums in and around Covent Garden, played a part in directing opinion towards the need for improvement—although Fielding, as a magistrate, was afraid that its immediate effect would be to give encouragement to those who might see themselves heroically mirrored in the underworld characters of the play.

Fielding's own revelations of the evil conditions appeared in the novels that he wrote after his career as a playwright was destroyed by the 1737 Licensing Act; and the opportunity to tackle the evils directly came to him when he was offered the post of Westminster magistrate. He installed himself in Bow Street in 1748, just a few weeks before the publication of *Tom Jones.*

Henry Fielding realised that crime and social deprivation were closely connected. And he came to the conclusion that crime had to be reduced to manageable proportions before the other problems could be approached effectively. The hard truth, however, is that for many years his advanced ideas on crime prevention, even with the evidence of highly successful experiments, were not followed through to provide any permanent improvement. Almost every important proposal the Fieldings made was shelved or rejected. Parliament and the people were more afraid of losing some apparent traditional freedoms than their purses or their lives.

Fielding wanted, above all, a unified mobile police force operating under a central direction that would concentrate on the suppression of crime. But almost to the end of his life the old system prevailed whereby anyone who assisted him in administration had to be paid out of the fees collected. Probably the most remarkable thing about the Bow Street Runners was that they

An aquatint after Pugin and Rowlandson showing a group of 'Charlies' preparing to represent law and order.

seriously pursued criminals instead of being concerned only with whatever easy rewards were to be picked up. Almost certainly this was due to the influence of Fielding's own character and example.

At that time the magistrates themselves lived on the fees they collected. Most of them were totally corrupt and known as 'trading justices'. One contemporary writer described them as 'low, needy mercenary tools who subsist on their commissions, hated and dreaded by the common people'. In this context Fielding's strict honesty and impartiality shone as a beacon in the darkness—and ensured for him a life hovering perpetually on the brink of ruin.

He pressed for measures to strengthen the power and authority of magistrates so as to increase their effectiveness in coping with crime; but property holders resisted these suggestions on the grounds that it would dangerously extend the powers of people appointed by the crown, and would endanger their own privileges.

Henry was already a dying man, his health undermined by his poorly rewarded efforts at Bow Street, when the Government ordered him, in 1753, to submit a plan for dealing with a particularly horrifying gang of murderers and robbers. They even went to the lengths of providing £600 for the operation.

The campaign was a brilliant success. What is more, there was money left over and Fielding used it to keep his chosen team of Runners together as a paid force. When this money ran out a successful application for more funds from the Treasury was made by John, after he had taken over from Henry at Bow Street. It was in this peculiar way that the Bow Street Runners became the first professional police force in England. The country could even sleep more easily at night in the knowledge that there were now two horses in constant readiness in Bow Street for pursuing criminals or galloping to the scene of a reported crime.

For a short while John also realised an ambition to have a horse patrol of the main highways around London, which could be summoned with horns by the turnpike clerks. But approval for this system was withdrawn after a year by the upholders of traditional arrangements.

With their training, experience and deep social commitment the Fieldings were able to assess clearly and define brilliantly the steps that were needed to arrest the eighteenth century plague of robbery and violence. And in due course the measures they suggested were put into effect, but only after many wasted years and many wasted lives.

Henry Fielding died in Lisbon in 1754, where he had gone in the hope of restoring his shattered health. John continued at Bow Street until his death in 1780, still seeking ways of putting Henry's ideas into effect. The city remained a place of widespread corruption and danger and at the end he only caught a glimpse of the dawning of the safer world that he and Henry had laboured long and desperately to establish.

Bow Street Police Station has its own way, and an excellent one, of reminding us of its illustrious progenitors. It houses the Metropolitan Police Historical Museum containing examples of police equipment and policemen's clothing in use since 1829. The museum is not open on Sundays, and admission at other times is by appointment. The latter aspect is simply a safeguard, however, and in practice it is usually possible for a visitor who applies to be conducted to the museum immediately.

Henry Fielding, after a portrait by Hogarth. Frustrated as a playwright and financially unsuccessful as a novelist, he became a magistrate at Bow Street and conceived the idea of a unified police force. But he died without seeing his plans fulfilled.

Theatre Royal, Drury Lane

The brilliant record in recent times of Covent Garden's two most celebrated theatres, the Theatre Royal, Drury Lane, and the Royal Opera House, can easily divert attention from the crucial part their arrival played in enhancing the status of the theatre in this country. This is especially true of the Theatre Royal, the creation of which was a landmark in the recovery of the drama from a condition close to total extinction.

Everything that had been achieved by Shakespeare at the Globe, and by the Elizabethan drama generally, was stamped underfoot when the Puritans came to power in 1642. Cromwell and his Parliament pulled down the theatres and branded all actors as 'a wicked sort of people' who should be 'taken as rogues'. Even spectators caught at illicit performances were fined and imprisoned or whipped.

A key figure in the reversal of the fortunes of the theatre was Sir William Davenant, playwright, Poet Laureate on the death of Ben Jonson, and in every way a man with the theatre in his blood. A possible clue is the widespread belief that he was a son of Shakespeare, who was known to be a frequent visitor to the Davenant household.

The first link in the chain of events that led to the creation of Drury Lane theatre, and with it the virtual rebirth of drama, was the possession by William Davenant of a Royal Patent to erect a theatre, which he had obtained from Charles I shortly before the disastrous arrival of the Puritans.

He joined the Court in Exile of Charles II and there met Thomas Killigrew, another dedicated man of the theatre. Then came the Restoration, and—mainly because of the charter from Charles I which Davenant had in his pocket—he and Killigrew were given a complete monopoly over the London theatre. This order of 1660 gave them the right to have companies, to build theatres, to exercise complete jurisdiction over them and to act as censors of all plays.

Davenant and Killigrew at first worked together in the revived Cockpit Theatre in Drury Lane, a tiny building that had been roofed over in 1616, the year in which Shakespeare died, and of

A tinsel picture, apparently of Edmund Kean, one of the great early-19th century actors at Drury Lane.

which Davenant had become Governor shortly before the arrival of the Puritans.

The Cockpit was, in fact, one of three spots in London where some acting had been carried on in spite of the constant persecution. At one point Davenant slyly exploited Cromwell's hatred of the Spaniards by putting on a production—with songs, dancing and words—advertised as 'The Cruelty of the Spaniards in Peru. Represented at the Cockpit in Drury Lane at three after noon punctually'. Painted backcloths were introduced in this production, and flats appeared in another anti-Spanish show that followed. Before long the two men went separate ways, Davenant went to

the old Duke's Theatre in Lincoln's Inn while Killigrew set about raising money for the building of the first Theatre Royal. Killigrew also made theatrical history at this time by presenting the first English actress on the professional stage. The role was Desdemona in *The Moor of Venice,* which opened at a theatre in Vere Street in December 1660, and evidence suggests that the actress was Mrs Margaret Hughes. Until then, of course, women's parts were invariably played by boys, but Killigrew broke the

This rare glimpse of an early (1697) Drury Lane performance showes the comedian Joe Haines delivering the epilogue to Tom Brown's The Unhappy Kindness *seated upon an ass.*

tradition, and his new theatre ensured that actresses had come to stay.

That first Theatre Royal was built on a corner site of Drury Lane surrounded by the aristocratic houses that then dominated the Covent Garden scene. The first of four that were built on the site, it was constructed mainly of wood and housed only 700 people, but it was very elegant and had two tiers of boxes including

One of the many theatre tickets designed by Hogarth for benefit performances put on to aid actors.

the splendid and appropriate innovation of a royal box. There was a proscenium arch and a curtain, but the front of the stage projected into the auditorium in the Elizabethan manner. The building had windows because most performances were then held in daylight, but there were also chandeliers with candles suspended from the proscenium arch, so that late performances could be staged. There were elaborately painted flats for scenery, but at first little or no stage furniture was used.

And so, on May 7, 1663, Thomas Killigrew opened the Theatre Royal with Beaumont and Fletcher's *The Humorous Lieutenant*. It was a boisterous event and a great success, signalling the complete acceptance of the new theatre by the people of London.

And on that day one member of the cast provided a fascinating link across the barren Protestant years, a link between the splendours of the Elizabethan stage and the new dramatic riches of the Restoration. He was Charles Hart, a grand-nephew of Shakespeare. Happily, he was also one of the greatest among many great actors of his time.

But the most significant aspect of the opening of this new theatre was the official support of the monarch. For the first time there was a Theatre Royal, and Killigrew's company was now 'The King's Company of Players' called upon to swear allegiance to the sovereign. All vestige of the old image of actors as little better or a little worse than vagabonds was swept away. The new theatre had all the security it needed to reinherit the dramatic kingdom.

The charter that was largely instrumental in bringing all this about is still in existence and must still be held by whoever holds the theatre. It is kept in the safe custody of the National Theatre Museum.

Tragically, the first building survived only nine years, including a year and a half when it was closed because of the plague, as were all places where crowds gathered. In January 1672 fire broke out beneath the stage and burned the theatre to the ground. A young actor, Richard Bell, died, too, when houses were blown up to confine the blaze.

The second theatre had to be simpler than the first as Tom Killigrew's resources were low, but it held around twice as many people and it was designed by Christopher Wren. The stage again projected well into the auditorium in a semi-oval, but there were now side wings instead of stage boxes.

This second theatre stood for 117 years, but it was then found to be unsafe and was demolished. The third was built by Sheridan. It ruined him eight years later, in 1809, when fire struck again and burned it down. It had been insured for only a fraction of its original cost of £250,000.

Then came the present theatre. Built by Benjamin Wyatt, it was opened in 1812, a year with well-remembered Napoleonic overtones. Part of the structure from the Wren building was incorporated, and still remains. The distinctive colonnade and portico were added later.

In the earliest days of the first Theatre Royal the enhanced status of the theatre was not echoed by the audience. The greatest moments of the most spellbinding actors might well be heard in rapturous silence, but that was all. Rich and poor alike went to the theatre in those days to be seen and heard as much as to see and hear. Wit was exchanged, with distance no barrier; finery was paraded, often with more dash than the stage itself could afford; commerce with prostitutes and haggling with the orange girls was conducted freely; quarreling and fighting were intermediate diversions; and bevies of beaux invaded the stage itself, so that the talents of the actors were stretched even to make an entry, let alone make an impression on the audience.

We surely owe something to the players of those times who insisted on making their lines audible above the din so that the drama could be kept alive in this country. And also something, perhaps, to the strange, mixed talent of the London audiences, which seemed to love the theatre as ardently as they strove to stifle it—comprehending in spite of everything and passionately applauding all that they found good.

One of the earliest notable names in the history of the Theatre Royal, Drury Lane, is that of Nell Gwynne. And if we care for the truth we should remember her first and foremost as a very fine actress, ignoring the popular misconception of the pretty miss who caught the eye of the King across a basket of oranges. The oranges were a short-lived expedient whereby a bright child of Covent Garden—with a drunken mother, no authenticated father and a longing to act—was able to get inside the theatre; and the fruit was far behind when Charles II succumbed to her enchantment as an actress.

Nell got her small foot on the first rung of the ladder to eternal fame when she joined the team of girls who sold oranges in the theatre under the eye of a privileged lady known as Orange Moll; and that was already an improvement on her earlier career as a child entrusted to fetch drinks for customers at a brothel—one run by a Mother Ross in a street off Drury Lane now called Macklin Street. Almost immediately on arrival she attracted the attention of Charles Hart, Shakespeare's grand-nephew, and they soon became lovers. He recognised her acting talent and helped to train her, and two years after the opening of the theatre she had the lead in a tragedy, *The Indian Emperor,* written by the Theatre Royal's first great dramatist John Dryden.

Nell was miscast in tragedy but splendid in comedy. The critical Pepys wrote of her Florimel in Dryden's *The Maiden Queen:* 'so great a performance of a comical part was never, I believe, in the world before.' The King was finally enslaved when she appeared in 1770, piquantly dressed as a young gallant, in a brilliantly performed prologue that devastated audience and actors alike. That night Covent Garden lost a daughter and the monarch gained a mistress.

Nell Gwynne held her King by and large to the end of his life. And with good reason. As well as being 'a mighty pretty soul' as Pepys described her, she was credited with natural grace, honesty and loyalty and a wonderful sense of humour.

A final flash of light that holds her brightly as a true and timeless Covent Garden product is the aside by Pepys after a rather bad night at the theatre—'to see how Nelly cursed for having so few people in the pit was very pretty.'

The fortunes of the Theatre Royal rose and fell through the years as playwrights and actors and actresses came and went and as managers coped or failed to cope with competition, slumps and

Nell Gwynne and the infant Duke of St Albans, by Sir Peter Lely, from the Denys Eyre Bower Collection, Chiddingstone Castle, Kent.

Left: The Theatre Royal as it appeared in 1775.
Below: Mrs Yates (1728-1787) as Calista in a Drury Lane production of The Fair Penitent.

other demons of the theatrical world. When Killigrew retired his two sons took over very unsuccessfully. Then an improvement came through a merger with the rival royal patent theatre off Fleet Street. The latter, built by Wren for Davenant's widow and sons and known as the Duke's Theatre in contrast to the 'King's Theatre' of Drury Lane, was originally a beautiful and splendidly equipped theatre, but it went to wrack and ruin and left the Theatre Royal as the only one with a royal patent. This brought to Drury Lane the remarkable Thomas Betterton, who introduced a restrained style of acting in place of the customary thumping and flailing, and earned from Pepys the simple commendation 'Mr Betterton is the best actor in the world.' With him was Edward Kynaston, who is remembered as perhaps the finest of the old school of male actors who played women's parts. Even though women, at the Lane, had well won their place on the stage, Kynaston was apparently still outstandingly brilliant at this speciality. Early leading ladies at the Lane were Anne and Beck Marshall, joined by Nell Gwynne and followed by Mrs Bracegirdle and Mrs Barry.

The Davenant brothers, when they took over the management in these bawdy times, introduced the works of Wycherley, Otway, Etherege, Sedley and Shadwell, as well as many more plays from Dryden. Rapacious Christopher Rich, who managed next, made no mistake when he took a play by a newcomer, William Congreve. This was *The Old Bachelor,* and its highly successful presentation was followed by *The Double Dealer.* Kynaston played Lord Touchwood, but his understudy took over one day in an emergency and began a long and notable career. He was Colley Cibber, who later became an actor-manager with Doggett and Wilks. He also wrote a play called *Love's Last Shift,* and a sequel to it was written by Sir John Vanbrugh—*The Relapse, or Virtue in Danger.* George Farquhar also contributed to this fertile period with *Love and a Bottle* and *The Constant Couple.*

For many people the name Drury Lane is virtually synonymous with spectacular, realistic drama, bearing in mind quite rightly the many lavish productions of this kind in the present century that incorporated lifelike effects such as the explosion of a ship, or a Zulu war. All this was uncannily foreshadowed in 1668 when a realistic play was staged called *Hide* (sic) *Park,* with live horses as a special attraction. Drury Lane managers soon realised and never forgot how readily the public will pay for the faithful representation on stage of sights that can be seen for nothing outside the theatre.

A threat to Drury Lane began to loom when Rich, at Lincoln's Inn Fields, exploited the growing popularity of operas and musicals, and it became more formidable still when his son, John Rich, who followed him, made a fortune by staging Gay's *The Beggar's Opera* in 1726 and spent it on a site in Bow Street where he erected the new Covent Garden Theatre Royal. He opened in 1732 with a revival of Congreve's *The Way of the World,* and went on to alternate plays with opera and ballet, aided by his close association with Handel.

But Drury Lane survived and prospered again. The persistence of Colley Cibber had rescued it from the avarice of Christopher Rich and introduced a fruitful partnership in management. After he retired it was taken by Charles Fleetwood, and he brought in James Quin from Covent Garden, a great actor in the grand manner. A further and major step forward was the arrival of Charles Macklin, who broke free from mannerism and gave a new meaning to the function of the actor. The first example of this was his portrayal of Shylock which had sunk into a low comedy role and which he now played with full regard for its human and tragic meaning. Other notable players of this time included Kitty Clive, a fine Portia for Macklin's Shylock, and Mrs Pritchard, famed for her Lady Macbeth.

Macklin outshone Quin but he in turn was outshone by a young man who hitch-hiked from Leicester with twenty-six-year-old Samuel Johnson and arrived at Drury Lane in 1742. David Garrick—it was none other—shed a great lustre on Drury Lane and the theatre generally during the next thirty years and more. He became joint manager and effected a theatrical transformation. In acting he completed the escape from cramping tradition, approaching every role afresh with powerful intelligence and deep insight. In the theatre he established order, removing the boxes from the stage and putting the actors back in full command in their own territory. He brought healthy discipline to rehearsals and nurtured the new spirit of naturalism. He instigated, after some hesitation, long-overdue reform in costume as part of the march towards realism. He appointed a musical director, Thomas Arne; and he gave to the world the first Drury Lane pantomime.

Peg Woffington was a comedy actress who came to Drury Lane at this time from Covent Garden. She was Macklin's mistress for a while and then became attached to Garrick. At one point all three lived together at No. 6 Bow Street. Macklin opted out first and then Peg and Garrick parted. He married after a while and lived for a long time in Southampton Street. Macklin was still acting when he was well over 90, and he haunted the piazzas and the streets of Covent Garden until he died, allegedly at the age of 107.

When Garrick reached the end of his career it was Richard Brinsley Sheridan who stepped in from the wings to take his place in the management of Drury Lane. Admirers of Garrick travelled from all over the country to attend his farewell performance, in *The Wonder,* in 1776. He then sold his half of the Royal Theatre Royal patent to Sheridan, who shared it with Thomas Linley and James Ford.

Great problems arose following the withdrawal of Garrick's organising genius, but the balance was magnificently redressed when Sheridan, following Garrick's advice to put everything possible into his writing, produced a play that he hammered into shape to exploit to perfection the individual talents of the existing Drury Lane company. This play was *The School for Scandal.* It was an immediate success and a landmark in the story of the Theatre Royal and British comedy. It saw the light on May 8, 1777, with Mrs Abington creating the role of Lady Teazle.

Another instance of success following something approaching disaster was the arrival of Mrs Siddons. She had her debut as Portia in 1775 and was a complete failure; but after seven years in the provinces she had learned enough to come back and take her place among the truly great actresses of Drury Lane. She was partnered by her brother, John Philip Kemble, who took over the management of the theatre in 1788. They were regularly together in *Macbeth* and many other notable productions.

The 19th century started with something of a bang at the Theatre Royal—an attempt on the life of George III whilst he was in the theatre. This piece of drama was a welcome failure.

One of the greatest actors of all broke upon the scene in 1814, making an immediate conquest with his first major role of Shylock. This was Edmund Kean. But he was a troubled, moody man, embittered by early poverty and the death of one of his sons. He drank heavily, brawled in the Covent Garden taverns, and was beset by a City alderman who discovered that Kean had been having an affair with his wife. All this, especially the drinking, finally defeated even his great talent and vitality and he died at the age of 46. In 1827, shortly before he died, his son Charles took to the stage and the name of Kean brought further lustre to the theatre in the ensuing years.

A much loved actor at this time was the wonderful clown Grimaldi. His own life became a tragedy, however, for he was overcome by a crippling disease and had to give up acting. In 1818, when he was destitute, a benefit performance was organised for him and although he had to be carried on to the stage, and performed sitting in a chair, he was still able to evoke laughter at will. The proceeds of £600 must have helped him for a long time.

In 1841 the great tragedian, William Macready, took over the management of the theatre as well for a few years, but lost money fairly heavily. This was a time when improved transport began to bring into London larger but less discriminating audiences, and new theatres were drawing the people in. Macready retired in 1851.

Soon after this the Theatre Royal began to create the special tradition that has characterised it ever since. It was started between 1863 and 1879 by F. B. Chatterton, who staged spectacular and realistic melodramas and pantomimes such as *The Great City*, with a real horse and cab, and *Formosa*, with an imitation boat race.

The pinnacle of prosperity for the Lane was reached during the reign of the theatre's greatest manager, Augustus Harris, who took over in 1879. There is one memorial to him in stone on the wall outside the theatre, and another in the name his generation gave to him—Druriolanus. He presented almost everything there was to present, including Shakespeare, grand and light opera, spectacular dramas, minstrel shows, and annual Christmas pantomimes of unexampled splendour. A feature of the pantomimes was the string of artists he recruited from the music hall, people like Vesta Tilley, Marie Lloyd, Dan Leno, Kate Vaughan and Fred Storey.

After Harris died in 1897 the tradition was carried on even more lavishly by Arthur Collins, until he retired in 1924. His audiences were regaled with the spectacle of divers under the sea, steam yachts passing through Boulter's Lock, a *Ben Hur* chariot race, an avalanche, an earthquake, and live horses racing neck and neck in *The Whip*.

There were also Shakespeare seasons given by Sir Henry Irving and Ellen Terry. Ellen Terry celebrated her stage jubilee in the theatre in 1905, a short while after Irving had completed his last London season. In 1916 Frank Benson was Julius Caesar in a Shakespeare Tercentenary performance, and after the performance he went into the Royal Box to be knighted by George V.

This brings us to territory that is familiar to many, and little more is needed to evoke the spirit of latter-day Drury Lane than such names as *The Garden of Allah, Rose Marie, The Desert Song,*

Land of Smiles, Noel Coward's *Cavalcade,* and Ivor Novello's *Glamorous Night, Careless Rapture* and *The Dancing Years,* followed by *Oklahoma, Carousel* and the musical that fittingly broke all previous Drury Lane records, *My Fair Lady.*

It would not be fair, and perhaps not altogether expedient, to leave the Theatre Royal, Drury Lane, without acknowledging the existence of its ghost. This man of all seasons has been seen by many people, including sober cleaning ladies—a young man in grey with costume, hat and powdered hair corresponding to a gentleman of the 18th century. His preference is for the upper circle during the day. Sometimes he watches rehearsals, and actors are sure that his appearances bring good luck.

The most likely theory is that it is the ghost of an unknown man whose skeleton, with a dagger in it, was found by workmen more than a hundred years ago in a forgotten bricked up room.

Joseph Grimaldi, the most famous of all clowns, sketched by a fellow-performer, T. M. Grimshaw, in pantomime garb for The Rival Genii.

The Royal Opera House

A lifetime of nearly seventy years elapsed between the opening of the Theatre Royal, Drury Lane and the opening of what is now The Royal Opera House, Covent Garden. It began with a revival of Congreve's *The Way of the World*, in 1732, and it heralded the beginning of a great rivalry between the two royally privileged theatres, and the Haymarket Theatre, that continued with varying intensity and oscillating fortunes until the time when they began to take distinctly separate paths.

Now, of course, The Royal Opera House exists as a home of opera and ballet, and Drury Lane tends to specialise in spectacular musical productions.

It is practically true to say that the entire history of English opera is the history of the Royal Opera House from the middle of the nineteenth century to the present day, its devotion to opera beginning in earnest in 1847 when the theatre was reopened, after structural alterations, as The Royal Italian Opera.

In the hundred years and a little more between the opening of the theatre and its dedication to opera, the actors who peopled the stage of the Royal Opera House were to a great extent those whose lives we have looked at in our study of the Theatre Royal, Drury Lane. They appeared on one stage or the other in response to a variety of pressures and the fluctuating fortunes of the two houses.

The excitement of the opening was caricatured by Hogarth in his famous print 'Rich's Glory', in which John Rich is seen entering his new theatre. He relished it as a triumphant restoration of the Rich's power in the land of Covent Garden following his father's ignominious expulsion from Drury Lane in 1711 by Colley Cibber.

The first theatre, known as the Theatre Royal in Covent Garden, was the most splendid that had yet appeared in London. Designed by James Shephard, it had a pillared portico and a particularly fine Amiconi ceiling. The early productions were spectacular—more so, in fact than those of its rival at the time—and they included pantomimes featuring John Rich as Harlequin.

There was a significant change of emphasis when Handel came from the Haymarket to join Rich, operas and ballets alternating

A robust Rowlandson contribution to the running battle with the Opera House administration—drawn in 1809, the year when the second theatre was opened to rioting over the new prices.

One of the memorable events of Covent Garden was the opening of the Covent Garden Theatre—now The Royal Opera House—on December 7 1732, when its creator, John Rich, entered it in triumph from his playhouse in Lincoln's Inn Fields. This print, questionably attributed to Hogarth, shows a procession approaching the entrance to the new theatre, which was then at the end of the colonnade. Rich, in the carriage, is dressed as the performing dog in

Perseus and Andromeda, John Gay, author of The Beggar's Opera *is on the back of a porter, and in the bottom right corner Alexander Pope is showing how much he 'dispises' the play. Nearby 'Another Author wheels his works, with Care, In hopes to get a Market at this Fair'. The crowd cries 'Rich for ever' and 'Gay for ever' reflecting a saying of the time that the* Beggar's Opera *made Gay rich and Rich gay—when 'gay' happily meant just what it said.*

with the production of plays. Between 1730 and 1741 the presentations of work by Handel included *Alcina, Alexander's Feast, Acis and Galatea, Esther, Samson, Judas Maccabaeus, Solomon* and, in 1743, *Messiah.*

Peg Woffington was among those who drifted over from Drury Lane. There came a time when she saw herself in danger of being outshone by the lovely George Anne Bellamy, and a moment in *The Rival Queens* when she was called on to stab her, with the words 'Die, sorceress, die!', proved too much of a temptation. Peg rolled her rival to the ground and beat her—scorning the requirements of the script—with the blunt handle of the dagger.

A lyric opera, *Artaxerxes,* by Arne, was the innocent cause of a disaster. Because of the high cost of its production the manager, John Beard, who had taken over in 1761, raised the admission prices. Modern audiences would show their resentment by staying away. Beard's audience did so by turning up and wrecking the place, causing more than £2000 worth of damage.

Disaster of a far worse kind struck in 1808, shortly after John Kemble had left Drury Lane and become a joint manager of Covent Garden. Fire broke out in the early morning of September 20 and destroyed the theatre completely. Handel's organ was lost, as well as all the jewels and other valuable items collected by Mrs Siddons; but even these losses were overshadowed by the tragic fate of 23 firemen who were killed when the roof suddenly fell.

Help came from all quarters and enough money was quickly raised to enable a new theatre to be built. Robert Smirke based his design on Athene's Temple on the Acropolis, with an impressive Doric portico and Flaxman bas-reliefs. This was opened in 1809, with *Macbeth.*

But toil and trouble was not confined to the stage. Kemble had put up the prices to help in covering the cost of the new theatre, and the audience again took strong exception. Placards and voices were raised and—mingling with every other conceivable sound—the chant was heard 'Old prices! No rise!' The 'O.P. riots' continued for several weeks and in the end Kemble gave in to the demands.

A theatrical landmark was registered in 1823 with a presentation of *King John.* In this production, by Charles Kemble, the actors wore mail armour and helmets that were completely authentic in appearance. The reception of this innovation was so enthusiastic that the way was cleared for the new era of stage realism which now swept into the London theatre.

Gas lighting was another innovation seen about this time, but it culminated in an explosion in the basement and a return to oil. There were other problems, including financial ones that brought the bailiffs to the door. There was a real danger that the theatre would be closed down for ever, but fate intervened at the last moment in true pantomime tradition. Quarrels at the Italian Opera

The 'cat engaged to squall' and 'John Bull with his bugle horn', from Rowlandson's Covent Garden satire 'The House that Jack Built'.

House in the Haymarket resulted in a decision by some of the rebels to buy the lease of Covent Garden theatre and convert it for full operatic productions.

However, a *Bal Masqué* at the end of a season of melodramas in 1856 finished at the break of dawn with another entry of the demon fire. In a short while there was practically nothing left of the theatre and, once more, it looked as though the end had come.

But yet again there were people who would not let the theatre die. Subscriptions were raised and the present theatre, designed by Edward Barry, was opened in 1858. It won universal admiration, with its Corinthian columns and the fine portico which served as a carriageway to enable the guests to alight under cover and proceed undampened up the grand stairway.

Grisi was already an established favourite at Covent Garden, and when she was about to retire in 1861 young Adelina Patti made a triumphant debut. But, after some splendid years, standards at the theatre declined and the situation was only saved by the arrival in 1888 of Augustus Harris—with ten years of success at Drury Lane behind him. Everything then prospered, and one of the crucial changes he introduced was the production of operas in the original language instead of only in Italian. This resulted in the name of the theatre being changed to the Royal Opera House. Among the singers that he introduced one of the best remembered is Tetrazzini.

When Harris died in 1896 control passed to the Covent Garden Syndicate, and during the splendid years up to the outbreak of the 1914-18 war audiences heard for the first time the voices of such singers as Caruso, Maggie Teyte, Martinelli and John McCor-

mack. They also saw the Russsian ballet of Diaghilev and never recovered from the impact. Nijinsky and Pavlova both danced during two visits by the company in 1911.

Between the two wars there were many problems but a constant succession of new productions and new singers such as Melba, Clara Butt, Eva Turner, Lotte Lehmann, Lily Pons, Kirsten Flagstad, Elisabeth Schumann, Joan Cross, Parry Jones, Lauritz Melchior, Richard Tauber, Heddle Nash, Gigli and Lawrence Tibbett.

Thomas Beecham and the Beecham Trust took a hand in trying to solve the financial difficulties, together with such groups as the London Opera Syndicate, the Grand Opera Syndicate and the Imperial League of Opera, but they could do little in the face of high costs and the difficulties that were besetting the nation as a whole.

At long last subsidies came to the rescue, the Covent Garden Opera Trust was formed and from 1947 on there was something approaching a sense of security. Then came Kathleen Ferrier, Victoria de los Angeles, Maria Callas, Joan Hammond, Boris Christoff, Tito Gobbi, Joan Sutherland, Jon Vickers and other great singers who played their part in transforming the theatre into one of the world's major opera centres.

Sir Thomas Beecham, who founded the British National Opera Company, has a secure place in this history not only for his great conducting but also for his legendary personality.

And the Royal Ballet took its place in the theatre, with Margot Fonteyn, Robert Helpmann, Nureyev and other great dancers drawing their own thousands of admirers from all over the world to the portals of Covent Garden.

Opera House Expansion

The magnificent productions of opera and ballet at the Royal Opera House have been mounted for many years in spite of cramped backstage conditions that were described more than ten years ago, by a Parliamentary sub-committee, as 'appalling'. With singers and dancers, and scenery and costumes, having to be whisked to and from centres and storage basements all over London and the Home Counties, almost every performance has been a near-miracle plucked from looming disaster.

All this is now in the process of vanishing into the realm of bad dreams through a programme of development to be carried out in two stages, the first due to be completed around 1982. This will create, at the back of the existing building, an opera studio, two ballet studios, a chorus room, dressing rooms and an opera wardrobe.

Thomas Allen as Papageno the bird catcher in Mozart's Die Zauberflöte *at the Royal Opera House. The first Covent Garden production of this opera was by a visiting German company in 1833.*

Later work, which could go on for another ten to fifteen years, may include the construction of rear and side stages to allow scenery to be moved on and off stage during performances—as can now be done at the new Metropolitan and in post-war opera houses on the continent. There will also be accommodation for the Royal Ballet School, a rehearsal room for the orchestra, built to recording studio standards, new workshops and administration offices, and spacious foyers and bars for the public.

The cost of the first phase alone will be nearly £8 million. More than half of this was raised in 1979 through private donations and grants from the Government and the Greater London Council.

The Royal Ballet

Major choreographic works from the past fifty years are now being revived at Covent Garden as a main feature of the 50th anniversary celebrations of the Royal Ballet, which completes its half-century in May 1981.

These revivals, which will continue to be presented at least until the end of the 1981 season, include a revised and refurbished production of *Swan Lake*, and revivals of *Giselle, A Wedding Bouquet, Les Biches and Cinderella*. The new production of *Swan Lake* retains the designs of Leslie Hurry and incorporates Frederick Ashton's choreography for Act IV.

Other ballets in the repertoire include *La Fille mal gardée, Manon, Mayerling, Romeo and Juliet, The Sleeping Beauty, The Concert, The Dream, Elite Syncopations, The Four Seasons, The Firebird, Four Schumann Pieces, Jazz Calendar, A Month in the Country, Les Noces, Scenes de Ballet, Les Sylphides, Symphonic Variations* and *Voluntaries*.

A new full-length ballet by Kenneth MacMillan and three new one-act ballets will also be staged during the 1980-81 season.

Performances are also given from time to time at the Royal Opera House by the Sadler's Wells Royal Ballet, the Royal Ballet's principal touring company, administered by the Royal Opera House. It returned to its former home at Sadler's Wells Theatre under its new name in 1977. Sadler's Wells Theatre, in Rosebery Avenue, near The Angel, Islington, is the theatre in which the Royal Ballet grew to maturity before moving to Covent Garden.

The 1980/81 season at the Royal Opera House will include a six-week 50th Anniversary Season with The Royal Ballet and the Sadler's Wells Royal Ballet.

The Sadler's Wells Royal Ballet has its own creative element. New ballets recently premiered include Kenneth MacMillan's

The Royal Ballet's prima ballerina Merle Park, as Countess Larisch, with David Wall, as Prince Rudolf, in the three-act ballet Mayerling *which brought Kenneth MacMillan the Evening Standard Award for the outstanding achievement in ballet in 1978.*

Playground and David Bintley's *Punch and the Street Party*. The current repertoire also includes *Coppélia, Papillon, The Grand Tour, Les Sylphides, Meadow of Proverbs* and *Pineapple Poll.*

The Royal Opera

The current season of opera at The Royal Opera House continues until mid-July, and the following season begins in October.

Productions during the early part of the 1979-80 season included the world premiere of John Tavener's *Thérèse* in October, *La Bohème, Norma, Così fan tutte, Die Fledermaus, La traviata, Werther, Eugene Onegin, Lohengrin, Lucrezia Borgia, The Rake's Progress, La Fanciulla del West* and *Die Zauberflöte.*

A new production of Verdi's *Simon Boccanegra* in June 1980 has Filippo Sanjust making his debut at the Opera House as designer and producer and Sir Colin Davis as conductor. The latter part of the 1979-80 season also includes *Tristan und Isolde* and *La Bohème.*

Transport Museum and Theatre Museum

The Flower Market building, fronting Wellington Street and Tavistock Street, has been allocated to the London Transport Museum and the National Theatre Museum, something that can be counted as a very valuable addition to the amenities of London as a whole. The London Transport Museum, which opened early in 1980, is on the strengthened ground floor; the National Theatre Museum is still to be installed at the time of going to press.

The Transport Museum

The London Transport exhibits, formerly in Syon Park, Brentford, show how London's transport system evolved and how the city and the suburbs grew as rapid transport became available. They consist mainly of road and rail vehicles that have been in use during the past century and a half. The road vehicles range from a reconstruction of George Shillibeer's horse-drawn omnibus of 1829 to the RT type bus of modern times, and include trolleybuses, trams and coaches. The impact of railways on London, both on the surface and underground, is illustrated in a number of displays. There is a steam locomotive that once pulled Circle Line trains and a coach from the very first 'deep tube' railway in the world.

The exhibition includes many working displays, most of which can be operated by visitors. One can work a 38 stock tube train controller and change a set of points laid out in a full-size section of tunnel segments. Other working displays deal with safety on the underground and give an impression of a signal cabin in operation.

Over the years London Transport has acquired a very high reputation for the artistic quality of its posters and there are many fine examples from its Poster Collection on view. Books, models and souvenirs can be bought in the shop and there is a coffee shop for light refreshments. The museum is open every day from 10am to 6pm, except Christmas Day and Boxing Day.

The National Theatre Museum

The National Theatre Museum is one of the happiest inspirations associated with the revitalisation of Covent Garden. There could be no better setting for it than the old Flower Market, practically within earshot of Drury Lane's Theatre Royal and the Royal

Many vehicles of this kind can be seen at the Transport Museum in Covent Garden.

Opera House, and surrounded by memories of theatrical triumphs and disasters and the actors and impresarios involved in them.

In substance the museum already exists, even before its installation in the Flower Market building. It came into being on September 16, 1974, as a new museum devoted to the performing arts, administered by the Victoria and Albert Museum under the Department of Education and Science. In Covent Garden it will be joined by collections formed by the British Theatre Museum Association and by the Friends of the Museum of Performing Arts.

What amounts to a complete history of the English stage from the end of the 17th century to the present day is embodied in the Gabrielle Enthoven Theatre Collection, which was first established in the V & A in 1925. It contains playbills, programmes, newspaper cuttings, letters, manuscripts, texts, prompt copies of plays, and libretti and music of operas and ballets. These are all arranged in date order under the names of the theatres where the performances took place. Visual material in this collection, which is kept up-to-date daily, includes engravings of scenes, portraits of performers, original drawings and designs, illustrated music sheets, architectural plans and views of theatre buildings, and an array of photographs dating from the mid-1850s to the present time.

Other collections complementing this material include the Guy Little Collection of historic photographs, the M. W. Stone Collection and Hinkins Collection of toy theatre sheets and play texts, the Nancy Price Collection of prompt books and the Melville Collection of Edwardian melodramas and pantomimes.

The ballet is well represented, firstly through the Ashley Dukes and Dame Marie Rambert Collection of engraved ballet portraits, the A. & C. Black Collection of modern ballet photographs, and the many programmes, photographs and books in the London Archives of the Dance. There is also the complete set of *Swan Lake* costumes used by the Russian Imperial Theatre and then by Diaghilev.

The latter is part of the drama archive and collection of designs recently acquired in its entirety from the Arts Council of Great Britain.

The Harry R. Beard Theatre Collection includes programmes, playbills, engravings and manuscripts relating to the British stage, as well as original drawings and designs, programmes and documents illuminating the history of opera and ballet in most European countries. Also in this collection are engraved portraits of composers, singers and dancers and views of foreign opera houses and theatres.

Among the many design exhibits are those for Wagner's *Ring* and other productions by Leslie Hurry, a large number of designs given by John Piper, and a collection of designs and other material relating to the Gilbert and Sullivan operas, presented by Dame Bridget D'Oyly Carte.

The broad scope of the museum provides a place for material relating to the music hall, the Gerald Morice Puppetry Archives, and the Antony Hippisley Coxe Circus Collection, which contains programmes, posters, photographs, engravings and drawings and an important collection of books dealing with the whole history of the circus.

Finally, there is a section covering the 'pop' cult, including badges, T-shirts, programmes and photographs. One of Elton John's more outrageous costumes is on view, as well as a broken guitar of Pete Townsend and some early stage clothes of the Beatles.

Anna Pavlova and a swan lake companion at their Ivy House home in Hampstead. The great dancer's well-documented career included dancing with the Diaghilev company at Covent Garden.

The Streets of Covent Garden

In the preceding pages much of the information is about Covent Garden in general. We now have in mind the special need that arises during active exploration—for descriptions that are brief enough to be read on the spot and broadly relevant to where one happens to be.

The first preoccupation is to make sense of the geography. The official maps place the boundaries roughly along High Holborn, Shaftesbury Avenue, Charing Cross Road, the Strand and a little way west of Kingsway. This is the outline we are using, too.

The maze of streets covering much of the area contributes a great deal to the charm of Covent Garden, but the abundance can be a little confusing unless a modest degree of order is introduced to the approach. An answer we offer is to divide the whole into four main sectors and then give a closer examination to the streets in each. We have decided, however, that it would not be practicable or very helpful to try to suggest a precise route that would take in every feature in a perfectly continuous sequence; the criss-crossing nature of many of the streets would make this a very demanding exercise indeed. We have grouped streets near each other together—and described each in its entirety—in a way that should accord with the tendency of the average traveller to follow as fancy dictates within an easily comprehended framework. There is no substitute for keeping one eye on the map.

The list on page 118 includes map references to the streets described in this section, and also has the page numbers of the street descriptions so that any one street can be located alphabetically.

The sectors have been chosen for ease of identification, using prominent through roads as dividing lines. The horizontal line is B402—Long Acre followed by Great Queen Street. The vertical line is B401—Endell Street, Bow Street and Wellington Street.

The four sectors which emerge are labelled North-West, North-East, South-West and South-East. The largest of these, the South-West Sector, includes very nearly all of Covent Garden's main identifying features—the square, St Paul's Church, the Market, the new museums, and the Royal Opera House. This sector will be

Lord Archer's House and the Piazzas as they appeared in 1796. The exterior of the house has survived and is regarded as one of Covent Garden's finest features.

dealt with first, followed by the two northern sectors and the South-Eastern Sector flanked by Kingsway.

Buildings stated as 'listed' are on the Statutory List or the Local List of buildings of architectural or historic interest.

South-West Sector

Covent Garden Underground Station is the arrival point for many visitors to Covent Garden, and this will accordingly be our starting point. Leaving Long Acre for attention later, we turn into James Street—which leads to The Piazzas, the old market buildings and St. Paul's Church.

James Street dates from the 1630s. The Nags Head, on the corner of Floral Street, has a history going back to the 1670's but the present building (listed) dates from 1900. Nos 21 to 31 are also listed.

Floral Street was created as a back street for the stables and coachhouses attached to the King Street residences. We hear of a cowhouse, dungheaps and brothels in the mid-nineteenth century—before it was known as Floral Street. Now it has some notable bookshops. At No 43 Bernard Stone, whom Laurence Durrell called 'the writer's friend', offers an eclectic selection of old and new poetry, fiction, children's and general books and private presses in an atmosphere of welcome informality. There are occasional small exhibitions of illustrations and prints, and all of the work of Ralph Steadman, the cartoonist/artist, can be seen here. The Dance Centre (11-14), opposite, includes a listed building and a swimming pool which won the Gold Medal Award in 1978 for the best designed pool and surround in the world. The Centre offers coaching in yoga as well as ballet, rock and tap. Nos 12, 33, 34, 46, 47 and 52 are listed.

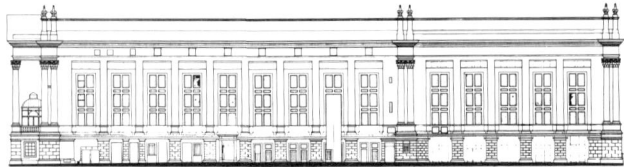

The Floral Street elevation of the Royal Opera House, including the extension—the section to the right—now being built.

Rose Street, which crosses Floral Street just before the Garrick Street end, is the narrow way where John Dryden was assaulted and severely beaten by three men on the night of December 18, 1679. He was most probably taking a short cut between Will's Coffee House and his home in Long Acre. The instigator is thought to have been the Earl of Rochester, who was annoyed by a satire about him which, mistakenly or not, he believed Dryden had written. Others have been blamed for the assault, including Louise de Kerouaille, mistress of Charles II, but with less credibility. The listed Rose Street pub The Lamb & Flag dates from the early 18th century but was refaced recently. It has a good 18th century staircase. The Samuel Butler who wrote the once-famous satire on Puritanism, *Hudibras,* died in poverty in Rose Street. Another resident, worth recalling if only for the aptness of his name as a publisher of obscene books, is Edmund Curll (1675-1747), referred to by some as 'the unspeakable Curll'. Nos 23 and 24 are listed buildings.

Garrick Street was built in the 1860s and named after the actor David Garrick. No 14 (listed), on the Floral Street corner has the impregnable Victorian-Methodist countenance of its original purpose as a mission house and school (1860). It has also been a stained-glass factory and is now the Inigo Jones restaurant. No 15, opposite, is the Garrick Club, founded in 1831 and used mostly by people from the theatre, law and the publishing professions. It was originally in 35 King Street and moved here in 1864. Another long-standing theatrical link is the shop of C. & W. May, the theatrical costumiers, at No 5 (listed). Other listed buildings are Nos 3, 5a, 7, 9, 11, 13, 14, 17, 19, 21 and 27.

King Street was laid out in 1633 in the grand manner as a fitting approach to the splendid Piazza. The original buildings were slowly replaced rather less ambitiously, but the spaciousness remained and in all the rebuilding there has been an obviously conscientious effort to maintain the tradition of elegance. Virtually all of the north side is listed as well as Nos 8, 14, 15 and 16 on the south side.

No 43, Thomas Archer House, is the finest of its kind in the whole of Covent Garden. The original building constituted the end one in the Piazza, and it was a worthy home for Admiral Edward Russell, the fourth Earl of Bedford's grandson. The present building which worthily replaced it in 1717 has changed much through the years inside, but the beautiful exterior has survived more or less intact. The house is named after its architect, who eventually inherited it after marrying into a branch of the Russell family. It became a hotel in 1772 and developed into an extremely fashionable one called the Star. It was then taken over by a Covent Garden theatre comedian W. C. Evans and became Evans' Hotel and Supper Rooms. One Paddy Green followed him and, in 1856, built a sumptuous music hall at the back of the house. It thrived for many years on the slightly bewildering policy of catering for 'steady young men who admire a high class of music, see no harm in a good supper, but avoid theatres and the ordinary run of music halls'. The performances were by men and boys, who sung glees and madrigals. Ladies were admitted grudgingly and allowed to see and hear from behind a screen. The National Sporting Club came into possession later—from 1891 until the thirties—the per-

A print sale in King Street, by Rowlandson.

formers still men but now delivering blows instead of ballads.

No 31 King Street was the birthplace of Thomas Arne (1710-78), who set many Shakespeare songs to music, composed operas and music for Milton's *Comus,* and who is associated more emphatically than fairly with bombastic renderings of his *Rule Britannia.* There is a praiseworthy delicacy of touch about the original setting of the piece as part of the masque *Alfred.* Here in Covent Garden it will be even more apt to think for a moment of the enchanting Shakespeare song 'Where the Bee Sucks . . .' This, and the other songs for *The Tempest* were written by Arne for a Garrick revival in 1746 at the Theatre Royal, Drury Lane, in which the part of Ariel was played by Kitty Clive.

In stark contrast to these reflections is the story of Arne in his King Street home—where his father was an upholsterer and coffin maker—practising on his violin with the music propped up on a coffin. It is said that the violinist Michael Festing, who found him doing this, remarked that he would not care to use a coffin as a desk for fear that it might contain a corpse. Arne merely lifted the lid to indicate that it did.

Arne's sister, also born at No 31, became Mrs Theophilus Cibber and also a celebrated actress and singer. David Garrick was a close neighbour for a short while, in 1748, at No 27. Much later, in 1801-2, Samuel Taylor Coleridge lived at No 10. Later again, in 1831, the Garrick Club began life at No 35.

Observant visitors may notice a substantial number of mahogany doors in King Street and elsewhere in Covent Garden. It was in a house in King Street where enthusiasm for this splendid timber, hitherto unknown here, first flourished. A supply came to England as ballast in a ship captained by the brother of a local physician, Dr. Gibbons. The captain gave some to the doctor, who persuaded a Long Acre cabinet maker, fearful of its effect on his tools, to make a bureau from it. Among visitors who called to see the piece in Dr Gibbons' King Street house was the Duchess of Buckingham, and her admiration for it triggered off the wave of popularity that mahogany has experienced happily ever after.

St Paul's Church is the focal point of the Covent Garden design conceived by Inigo Jones at the instigation of the Fourth Earl of Bedford. It was built between 1631 and 1633. The exterior has survived without essential change, but a spectacular fire in 1795 destroyed the interior. The restoration and subsequent work involved raising the chancel and blocking up the east doors facing into the square. St. Paul's is known as the actors' church, but although the theatrical connection is strongest it has an unbroken association with the arts generally. Those buried in the precincts include Sir Peter Lely, William Wycherley, Thomas Rowlandson, Thomas Arne, Charles Macklin and Ellen Terry. A large number of theatrical people have memorial panels inside the church. The impressive portico has two special associations. A Punch and Judy show took place there on May 9, 1662, watched by Samuel Pepys—who brought his wife to see it two weeks later. This event is commemorated each year with a puppeteers' service and May Fayre. The other event, though a fictitious one, is real enough to theatre-goers and those who admire the musical version of Bernard Shaw's *Pygmalion*, the widely-acclaimed *My Fair Lady*. The portico is the spot where Professor Higgins first saw and heard, in anguish, Eliza Doolittle. For a fuller account of St. Paul's church, see the earlier chapter devoted to it. (p. 27).

The Market. The Central Market building, now called simply The Market, was built in 1828-30 under a special Act of Parliament to replace the former unsightly conglomeration of structures that had grown up as part of the fruit and vegetable market all over the square. The designer, Charles Fowler, provided Tuscan columns, a triangular pediment and arcades that would blend with St. Paul's church and the Piazzas. The glass roof was added by the builders, William Cubitt, nearly fifty years later. Over the years the market clutter obscured much of the inherent beauty of this building, but it can now be seen and enjoyed to the full again following the removal of the fruit and vegetables to Nine Elms, south of the river, and the restoration that has been carried out with care and sympathy by the GLC Historic Buildings Board. The shops, restaurants and other services in The Market are listed elsewhere.

Jubilee Market. This structure was built on the south side of the square in 1904 to house the trade in vegetables and imported flowers. The upper floor recently became a temporary sports hall and the lower area was taken by stallholders selling a wide variety of wares. Plans to demolish this building have met with a great deal of opposition.

Flower Market. Built in 1872 for the flower trade, this listed building facing Wellington and Tavistock Streets has been converted and strengthened to house the Transport Museum and the National Theatre Museum. Details on page 69.

The Piazzas. The sensational success of the Covent Garden scheme when it first appeared on the London scene was due in no small measure to the effect of the Piazzas. Inigo Jones wanted the arcades to run most of the way round the square, but the need for economy confined them to two sides. Even this was enough to achieve his object of creating the atmosphere of an Italian piazza. The Covent Garden square was, itself, originally referred to in its entirety as The Piazza, but the name eventually became associated only with the arcades. The present Piazzas are an approximate reproduction of the original work. The buildings that preceded the present arcades have housed or known many notable people, including the artists Sir Peter Lely, Godfrey Kneller, Richard Wilson and William Hogarth, and the theatrical people Thomas Killigrew and Charles Macklin.

The north-east corner was once occupied by the *Shakespear Tavern*, where James Boswell, on one occasion, repaired with two girls of the street and 'solaced my existence with them, one after the other, according to their seniority'. And in a house to the rear of it John Rich, actor, manager and theatre-builder, lived for many years in the mid-18th century.

Close by was the Great Piazza Hotel. Richard Brinsley Sheridan went there for a glass of wine after watching his Theatre Royal, Drury Lane, being destroyed by fire—and drank it, it is said, with the comment: 'A man may surely be allowed to take a glass of wine at his own fireside'. Charles Dickens stayed there later, in 1844 and 1846, by which time it was the Piazza Hotel. It was visited by Steerforth in *David Copperfield.*

Next door to the corner-sited *Shakespear Tavern*, on the Russell Street side, stood the Bedford Coffee House, one of the most favoured of the establishments of its kind where writers, actors, dramatists and fellow spirits congregated after performances. They included David Garrick, Sheridan, Oliver Goldsmith, Henry Fielding, Horace Walpole, the actors Macklin and Quin and the poets William Collins and Pope. A little to the south of the Russell Street corner was the site of the first Turkish baths established in this country—called a 'bagnio' or 'hummums'. Later it became a hotel called the Hummums.

Russell Street. In this street there were three well known coffee houses, Button's, a few yards down on the right (No 10), Tom's almost opposite, and Will's on the corner of Bow Street.

Button's Coffee House was opened in 1712, Daniel Button himself having been set up in business by Addison of the *Spectator,* or by his wife, the Countess of Warwick. Those who frequented Button's with Addison included Pope, Swift and Steel. A feature of the place was the Lion's Head, a letterbox so shaped, for the receipt of news and gossip for one of Addison's publications named the *Guardian*—not an ancestor of the present one.

Tom's Coffee House, on the site of No 10, was opened in 1700 by Captain Thomas West, who was plagued by gout to such an extent that he finally threw himself out of a second floor window to his death. It was taken over by Thomas Baines, a polished gentleman, and his regular guests included Dr Johnson, Smollett and Fielding. A club formed there in 1764 included the Duke of Northumberland, the Marquis of Granby and Earl Percy amongst its subscribers, as well as Garrick and Oliver Goldsmith.

Will's was the most popular of all the coffee houses. It was established in 1671, and its reputation was made and maintained by the constant presence of John Dryden for something like forty years. During the winter he presided from a chair by the fire and

A contemporary impression of one of the hazards facing the nocturnal reveller 'Going Home from Tom King's Coffee House'.

in the summer he moved his court on to the balcony. People came from far and wide to see him and to catch passing shafts of his celebrated wit; his audiences included politicians, lords and scholars as well as literary men such as William Wycherley, Alexander Pope and Pepys.

No 8 Russell Street, a listed building, witnessed a meeting that had far-reaching consequences. It was the first encounter, in the bookshop of Thomas Davies, between Dr Samuel Johnson and James Boswell. Charles Lamb and his sister Mary were at No 20 from 1817 to 1823, and on Wednesdays they had literary evenings there. Lamb wrote some of the earlier *Essays of Elia* at this time.

On the other side of Bow Street, just outside the sector we are dealing with at the moment, Russell Street runs along the side of the Theatre Royal, Drury Lane; and on the north side of the street there is the small *Fortune Theatre*, built in 1924.

Henrietta Street came into existence in 1631 and was named after Charles I's queen. The Castle Tavern, which formerly stood on the corner of Bedford Street, on the north side, was the scene of a duel between Sheridan and a Captain Matthews who had written something unpleasant about Sheridan's future wife, Miss Linley.

Rowlandson's 'The Mad Dog in the Coffee House', which offers a richly extravagant glimpse of coffee house life in his time.

The architect of the present building (1858), Charles Gray, was partly responsible at the age of 18 for the birth of the Architectural Association. Jane Austen's brother was a partner in a bank that occupied No 10 from 1807 to 1816. He lived above it, and Jane sometimes stayed there. In 1819 a proposal of marriage arrived at No 8 from lovelorn Charles Lamb addressed to the beautiful actress Frances Maria Kelly—said to be the first woman solo performer. She did not hesitate. She sent back a refusal the same day. Washington Irving stayed with a friend for some time at No 22 in 1824. The magazine proprietor C. Arthur Pearson developed his business in Henrietta Street, and several other publishers have dwelt in it. Victor Gollancz can still be found at No 14. Nos 3 to 10 and 22 to 32 are listed buildings, including St. Peter's Hospital, which moved there from Marylebone in 1882.

Maiden Lane. The origin of the name is unclear but one possibility is that evolved from its mid-way position (midden) between the Strand and the market. It has illustrious associations. J. M. W. Turner, the artist, was born in 1775 in the house of his hairdresser father (No 21), and they also lived later at No 26. Poet Andrew Marvell was at No 9 in 1677 in a state of poverty shortly before his death. During his exile in England Voltaire lodged at a house in Maiden Lane, in 1727, where he was visited by Congreve, Walpole and Pope. Another occupant, in 1663, was William Bancroft, later Archbishop of Canterbury. The depths of No 21 once contained the Cider Cellars, a place of greater distinction than the name suggests judging from the people who graced it such as Benjamin Disraeli, William Makepeace Thackeray and Louis Napoleon.

No 35 houses the celebrated (and listed) Rules Restaurant, much used by actors and writers, and with a wonderful atmosphere. Playbills, cartoons, reproductions and souvenirs of the theatre adorn its walls. The business is said to date from 1798, and most people are convinced that Edward VII entertained Lily Langtry in an alcove on the first floor. Nos 16-20 are listed buildings.

Lumley Court, Bull Inn Court and **Exchange Court** are alleyways between Maiden Lane and the Strand that were once beloved of footpads and cut-throats. Bull Inn Court saw the sad end of a hero of the Adelphi Theatre, William Terris, described by Ellen Terry as a heaven-born actor 'who had unbounded impudence, yet so much charm that no one could ever be angry with him'. He was killed by a demented stage-hand with an imaginary grievance.

It makes sense at this point to walk into the Strand and look at the Adelphi Theatre and its close neighbour the Vaudeville.

Mrs Patrick Campbell, for whom Shaw wrote the part of Eliza Doolitle in Pygmalion. *Admiring her greatly as a person, he also wrote her an entire volume of letters.*

The Adelphi Theatre, which opened in 1930 with the C. B. Cochran musical *Evergreen,* is the fourth to have been built on the site, disregarding the passing on of remnants. The first began life in 1806 as the Sans Pareil, offering the world *Miss Scott's Entertainment.* The second opened as The Theatre Royal, New Adelphi, in 1858. The third was originally called the Century Theatre, and its opening production in 1901, *The Whirl of the Town,* is a nostalgic reminder that the Strand was the centre of the entertainment world at the turn of the century.

The present theatre housed many Cochran productions in its early years. A recent major event of special significance in relation to Covent Garden was the highly successful revival of *My Fair Lady.* A long run is still predicted at the time of going to press.

Mrs Patrick Campbell, for whom Shaw later wrote the part of Eliza Doolittle, emerged from the ranks of the unknown at the Adelphi when she was 'spotted' in a drama called *The Trumpet Call* and offered the part of Paula in Pinero's new play *The Second Mrs Tanqueray.*

The Vaudeville Theatre originally opened in 1870 and has since been twice reconstructed—in 1891 and 1926. It is now one of London's most charming small theatres, with a seating capacity of 659.

Bedford Street. The father of Richard Brinsley Sheridan had a house on the corner of Bedford Court that looked down Henrietta Street, and this favoured viewpoint resulted in a cherished record of his friend Dr Johnson walking the length of it on his way to dinner, 'working along with a peculiar solemnity of deportment' and laying his hand deliberately on each of the anti-carriage posts standing at regular intervals along the street. He even went back to include one he had accidentally missed.

Many publishers were here in the 19th century. *Alice in Wonderland* came from Macmillan at No 16 in 1865, and about a year later the Peter Rabbit stories of Beatrix Potter began to emerge from Warne at No 15. Dents came to No 29 in 1898 and launched their famous Everyman Library. *The Lady* magazine, at Nos 39/40, was launched in 1885.

Far-famed Moss Bros., at 21–26, dates from 1860, when a shop was opened at No 25 by Moses Moses. The business of hiring out formal dress developed into its present magnitude out of a modest transaction in 1897 with an amateur entertainer, Charles Pond, who became addicted to borrowing a suit for use at weekend house parties.

Southampton Street took the place of Bedford House after the latter was pulled down in 1704 or thereabouts. Two of the original houses in the street are still standing, Nos 26 and 27, both listed buildings. No 27, Garrick House, is where that great actor David Garrick lived from the time of his marriage in 1749, to the dancer Eva Maria Violetta, until 1772. No 17 is regarded as the birthplace

A portrait of Garrick, from life, by J. K. Sherwin.

of W. S. Gilbert, the librettist of the Gilbert and Sullivan light operas. And yet another occupant of Southampton Street was the actor Colley Cibber.

No 26 is the home of the firm of Samuel French, treasure chest of acting editions for the entire theatrical world. The business was started in nearby Wellington Street in 1830 by a Thomas Lacy when he was only 20, and he sold out in 1872 to Samuel French, who had been running a similar business in America but found that London was better for his health than New York.

Tavistock Street is named after a seat of the Bedford family. The Country Life Building, Nos 2-10, was designed in 1905 by the leading architect of his day, Sir Edwin Lutyens. Nos 34 to 38 are worthy survivors from 1733. Thomas De Quincey wrote his *Confessions of an English Opium Eater* in a room at the back of No 36. The portion of Tavistock Street beyond Catherine Street, known earlier as Russell Court, once contained the Star Tavern. Its accommodation was good enough to attract such a distinguished guest as Casanova but it failed in its efforts to find him a bedfellow to his liking.

The famous auctioneers Sotheby's grew out of a bookshop in Tavistock Street that started a saleroom in the mid-18th century. Listed buildings are Nos 11-19, 26-28, 32-42 and 2-10.

Exeter Street. Dr Johnson lodged in a house at the Wellington Street end in 1737 during his early days in London. A report of 1842 refers to the annoyance caused by a brothel in the street from which screams emerged 'throughout the greater part of the night' while in the yard 'Women in a state of almost perfect nudity are

The Royal Opera House entrance in the year 1860.

constantly exposing themselves'. Was there a speedy improvement or was it scientific detachment that, nine years later, permitted the opening close by of the Royal Panopticon Institute of Science? Listed buildings are No 15, No 17—formerly the Victoria Club—and the Old Bell Tavern.

Burleigh Street was started by Lord Burleigh in 1673, and the upper part was added in the mid-19th century. No 14, a listed building, was erected in 1860 to serve St Michael's Church that once stood nearby but was pulled down in 1906. It is now the St Paul's rectory.

Wellington Street was completed in 1835 and named after the Duke of Wellington. Charles Dickens worked at No 26 and launched a weekly newspaper there in 1850 entitled *Household Words* which published *Hard Times* serially. Its successor, *All The Year Round*, also published in Wellington Street, ran *A Tale of Two Cities* and *The Uncommercial Traveller*.

The Lyceum Theatre has had an erratic career, opening for varied forms of entertainment in 1772 and becoming the English Opera House in 1809. The great years of the Lyceum began when Henry Irving became manager in 1878 and took Ellen Terry as his leading lady. His sensational role in *The Bells* then saved the theatre from disaster but his departure with Ellen Terry in 1902 brought doom at last. The 1831 portico survives from the fourth building on the site, and the future is hazy.

Bow Street, so named because of its curved shape, holds much that is vital and memorable in Covent Garden. The obvious starting point is the Royal Opera House, and attending a performance there is the truest initiation into the magic of this place. A sense of the past will be a part of the experience and this should lead naturally to a wish to know something about that past. The brief notes here can provide only an outline. Earlier pages deal with the connected story of the two Royal patent theatres—the Theatre Royal, Drury Lane, and the Royal Opera House.

The first theatre on the Bow Street site was built in 1732 and destroyed by fire in 1808. Its successor went the same way in 1856 after setting the stage for the future by operating for nine years as the Royal Italian Opera House. The present theatre, designed by E. M. Barry, opened in 1858 and has changed little since, until the present extension scheme was set in motion to bring the backstage facilities into line with modern needs.

Barry was also the architect responsible for the adjoining Floral Hall, in cast iron and glass, built by the theatre owner, Frederick Gye, and used for a bizarre combination of concerts, balls, skating and 'a splendid collection of flowers of every kind, all of which are marked for sale in plain figures'. In 1865 the Duke of Bedford stopped the music and put the hall to use for auctioning fruit. It is a listed building.

In the theatre, a 'Golden Age of Opera' flourished under the

Grand Opera Syndicate from 1896 until the outbreak of World War I. And the seeds of future balletomania were sown when they brought the Russian Ballet to London in 1911. After World War II the ballet company raised in London by Ninette de Valois became the Royal Ballet and took its place in the theatre alongside the Royal Opera.

Bow Street's second claim to wider than local fame is its association with the Bow Street Runners—and with the Fieldings in their role as magistrates. Here, again, the more substantial account that appears earlier should be read to do them full justice. But it can be said, briefly, that Henry Fielding, the author of *The History of Tom Jones*, became a Justice of the Peace in 1747 and ran his court at (vanished) No 4 Bow Street in an honest and caring manner that

The Floral Hall, which was added to the Royal Opera House during the enthusiasm for iron and glass structures evoked by the Crystal Palace. It was opened on March 7 1860 with the Volunteers' Ball, splendidly depicted in the illustration of the interior below, right.

started the upward climb of the British judicial system from its traditional morass of corruption. He had advanced and passionately-held ideas on crime-fighting which were almost totally rejected whilst he was alive and quickly adopted after his work-hastened death. He was aided and succeeded by his blind half-brother John, and their dream of a permanent, salaried police force—in place of the sporadic use of free-lances paid out of proceeds—became reality in the shape of the first, fine team of Bow Street Runners. The Court moved from No 4 to the present (listed) building, opposite the Opera House, in 1880.

The house that was next door to Fielding's, No 6, was probably the one which David Garrick and actor-manager Charles Macklin shared together with the love of the beautiful actress from Dublin,

Peg Woffington. Others who lived in Bow Street included William Wycherley, Thomas Arne and the sculptor Grinling Gibbons.

It is worth recalling that the Cock Tavern once stood opposite the theatre, if only for the fact that a record of a night in 1663 gives us another of those sudden glimpses of life as it was sometimes lived in Covent Garden. After a long drinking session three friends, including a future earl, Charles Sackville, appeared on the balcony of the tavern and decided to deliver a lecture to onlookers below, removing all their garments to allow them to illustrate their theme, whatever it was, with unmistakable mime and gesture. They were mobbed by the onlookers, rescued by the police and heavily fined by the magistrate. And, finally, it is rumoured that an all-forgiving monarch, Charles II, paid the fines.

Broad Court was rebuilt to a great extent at the end of the 19th century, and includes the Fielding Hotel. No 5 and Nos 11-19 are listed buildings.

Long Acre is the central artery of Covent Garden. Each morning during the years of the fruit and vegetable market it was a narrow way crammed with laden and bellowing mammoths, sliding in, unloading and slipping miraculously out again, attended by rope-throwing, basket-juggling acrobats. Now it is all for shoppers, a lively thoroughfare with much to arrest the window-gazer and browser. One can linger endlessly in such places as the Arts Council Shop, packed with books, programmes, posters, slides and similar items, or in nearby Stanford's, where there is a galaxy of books for travellers and a universe of maps in all scales and sizes. Or in shops flowing with herbal perfumes, bright utensils, craft products from Africa and the Orient and similar tempting objects.

When the monks were tending their convent garden this street was a path through a narrow field to the north of it. The field was eventually called Seven Acres, and Long Acre was the name that came to be applied to the thoroughfare. By 1650 it was a street of small shops such as grocers and chandlers, with a few big houses here and there.

Dryden lived on the north side opposite Rose Street, and William Hazlitt was next door for a while about a century later. Oliver Cromwell is thought to have stayed somewhere on the south side for a few years around 1640.

Long Acre became the centre for coach and carriage making in the 18th century, before fruit and vegetable wholesalers moved in.

These are the listed buildings: Numbers 10, 12, 13, 14, 22, 23, 30, 31, 44, 48-55, 61, 66, 78, 79, 100-104, and 116.

St Martin's Lane can be followed in the knowledge that it is one of the oldest thoroughfares in the district. It was probably in existence in the 13th century, or earlier, as a footpath and later as a lane between St Martin in the Fields and St Giles in the Fields.

Many artists and other illustrious people have been associated with St Martin's Lane. Inigo Jones lived at No 31, and a drawing academy near the Duke of York's Theatre—a forerunner of the Royal Academy—was attended by Hogarth, Reynolds, Hayman, Cipriani, Ramsey, Cosway and Nollekins, to name a few.

Old Slaughter's Coffee House once stood on the corner with Cranbourn Street. Established in 1692, it became a favourite resort of artists, sculptors, wits and others, including Gainsborough, Wilkie, Roubiliac, Pope, Dryden, Boswell and Hogarth. The last was a particularly frequent visitor as he lived nearby in Leicester Square.

The famous furniture-maker Thomas Chippendale had his first workshop at No 60, and Josiah Wedgwood once had a showroom and residence at the Great Newport Street junction. Other St Martin's Lane residents included the painter Henry Fuseli at No 100, the engraver John Pine at 88-9, and Ellen Terry at No 34.

Listed buildings include Nos 30, 31, 32-36, 38, 39, 52-54, 58 (Angel & Crown), 62, 77-81, 82-84, 89-93, and all three theatres.

St Martin in the Fields Church, built in 1722-24, is regarded as the finest example of the work of James Gibbs. The interior includes a fine ceiling by Artari and Bagutti, a font of 1689 from the previous church and, in the crypt, a whipping post and the old parish chest made in 1597. Bacon, Hampden and Charles II were christened here, and burials recorded include those of Nell Gwynne, Farquhar and Chippendale.

St Giles in the Fields is well outside the usual Covent Garden boundaries, but it is too closely related to the area to be ignored completely. It was built in 1731-33 by Flitcroft and restored in 1954. It contains a Father Smith organ of 1671, a pulpit of 1676, and part of a later pulpit used by John and Charles Wesley.

A strong theatrical tradition is enshrined in the continued presence in St Martin's Lane of three important theatres, the Coliseum, the Duke of York's and the Albery.

The Coliseum, originally called the London Coliseum, opened with variety in 1904. It is one of the largest theatres in London and has a capacious stage in three sections forming concentric revolving rings. In 1968 it became the home of the Sadler's Wells Opera Company, renamed the English National Opera in 1974.

The Albery Theatre was opened in 1903, as the New Theatre, with the play *Rosemary*—not to be confused with the later musical *Rose Marie*. During the Second World War the theatre became the headquarters of the bombed-out Old Vic Company and the Sadler's Wells Ballet. The ballet eventually transferred to Covent Garden, and from 1945 to 1949 the Old Vic Company continued alone at the New and enjoyed four years of tremendous success, with Laurence Olivier and Ralph Richardson as leading actors. The name Albery was adopted in 1972, commemorating Sir Bronson Albery, manager of the theatre during the Thirties.

The Duke of York's Theatre, originally the Trafalgar Square Theatre, was the first theatre in St Martin's Lane, opening in 1892 with the comic opera *The Wedding Eve*. It is relatively small, seating 700, and had a new scheme of decoration in 1950 designed by Cecil Beaton. Productions have included many Noël Coward successes.

Chandos Place, formerly Chandos Street, was named after a family connected by marriage to the 4th Earl of Bedford. On the south side, near the corner with Bedford Street, there was formerly a blacking factory that for a time employed a very unhappy 12-year-old boy, Charles Dickens. His father and mother were in prison for debt and he was sent to work there, walking every day from his lodgings in Camden Town. In those hard times he found something consoling about Covent Garden, and began to love it. 'When I had no money', he said, 'I took a turn in Covent Garden and stared at the pineapples.'

Nearby once stood the Three Tuns, visited often by Pepys, and also by a certain Sally Salisbury, described in 1723 as 'the most notorious woman that ever infested the Hundreds of Old Drury or Covent Garden either.' It no doubt had something to do with the fact that she stabbed the Honourable John Finch. And a little earlier, in the 17th century, Mother Maberley ran the Hole-in-the-Wall on the site of the present Marquis of Granby—a hole that failed to provide a safe refuge for highwayman Claude Duval, who was arrested there in 1669. Listed buildings are the Marquis of Granby and Nos 44, 60, 66, 67 and 68.

The entire triangle formed by **William IV Street, Adelaide Street** and the connecting section of the Strand is listed because of its architectural quality. Charing Cross Hospital to the north is now a refuge for the destitute, and has a listed frontage on **Agar Street.** Rhodesia House, on the corner of the latter with the Strand, has sculptures by Jacob Epstein, and is also listed.

In the **Strand,** on the corner of Bedford Street, is a notable landmark, the Civil Service Stores. It owes its origin to a few Post Office clerks who bought and shared a chest of tea in 1864. This taste of the heady bulk-buying brew led them to create an organisation which extracted similar economic advantages from other goods, and extended the privileges to other members of the Civil Service. All membership restrictions were eventually lifted, and the store is now a normal one with no link whatever with the Civil Service. The present store was built in 1877 and given a £1 million 'facelift' in 1978.

Of the several courts attached to St Martin's Lane the most picturesque is **Goodwin's Court,** which has some fine (listed) 18th century shop-fronts. Mozart lodged in **Cecil Court** in 1764. **Hop**

Many flamboyant characters of the theatre are now almost forgotten, such as Alice Atherton, captured vividly here as a clown in the 1880s. We know only that she appeared at Toole's Theatre, once standing near Charing Cross.

Gardens needs no more than an answer to the obvious question. There was, in fact, a hop garden nearby in the 17th century.

New Row started life in 1635 and still has some 17th and 18th century buildings. John Flaxman, the sculptor, once lived there and Dr Johnson 'dined very well for eightpence' at the Pine Apple, apparently quite often. The White Swan pub is listed, as well as Nos 1-10, 13, 16-18, and 21-25.

Bedfordbury has on one side of it the Peabody Estate, built in 1881. Its creator was the American philanthropist, George Peabody, whose ancestors went from Leicester to New England in 1635. After making a fortune from dry-goods stores in America, he became a banker in London in 1843. It is not easy to appreciate the great contribution he made with the buildings that he provided for the poor in various parts of Covent Garden and elsewhere in London, but there is plenty of proof that most of the inhabitants have lived very happily in them and will not hear a word against them. And the drabness of his multi-memorial can be forgiven in the light of the knowledge that his generosity was abundant in many directions, that he promoted Anglo-American friendship, and refused an English baronetcy. There are three listed buildings at the north end of the street, Nos 23, 24 and 25.

Charing Cross Road, though a Covent Garden boundary line, cannot be regarded as a true part of it. Nevertheless it has important interests for visitors, including its bookshops and theatres. **Wyndham's Theatre,** with a capacity of 760, opened in 1899. Its façade, in classical style, was designed by W. G. R. Sprague **The Garrick Theatre** was financed by W. S. Gilbert and opened in 1889 with Pinero's *The Profligate*. It still has the original gallery and generally retains the atmosphere of a Victorian playhouse. The portrait of Garrick in the foyer is a copy of one by Gainsborough that has been lost. This can serve as a reminder that the **National Gallery** and the **National Portrait Gallery** are just across the road. Naturally, many of the people who were associated with Covent Garden have a place in the Portrait Gallery.

Cranbourn Street has several buildings on the Local List. They are Nos 26-34.

In **Great Newport Street** The Frigate pub, formerly the Cranbourn, is on the Statutory List, also the building next to it, No 5. The Photographer's Gallery, further along, has exhibitions of great interest to all who enjoy photographs as well as to practising photographers.

The Arts Theatre, occupying Nos 6 & 7 Great Newport Street, is a small club theatre with pleasant facilities for members at a relatively modest subscription. Temporary membership is available for theatre attendance only. The theatre was opened in 1927 but its early years were inauspicious. Then the Arts Theatre Group of Actors was founded by Alec Clunes in 1942 and its work gained it a reputation of comprising a 'National Theatre in miniature'. Now, as well as presenting new plays and revivals for adults, it is building an international reputation for developing an interest in the theatre amongst children, through the Unicorn Theatre Club. This is a professional theatre presenting plays and theatre workshops for children between four and twelve every weekend and during school holidays. The young members learn about improvisation, scene-painting, tumbling, puppet-making, music, make-up and magic. Concerts, films and puppet shows are presented in addition to plays. Children can join for a year, four months or just one performance.

North-West Sector

The distinctive feature of this sector, as a glance at the map will show, is the group of streets radiating from **Seven Dials.** A second look will show that this complex is very much like a flag—the Union Jack—with streets running along each edge of the rectangle. Remembering this fact can be an aid to orientation.

The neat Seven Dials plan was the brain-child of Thomas Neal, Master of the Mint at the end of the 17th century, and the name is an acknowledgment of the fact that there was originally a column with sundials at the top of it at the point from which the seven streets radiated. The column had a moral-folk-tale end. In 1773 everyone became convinced that there was treasure buried beneath it and it was taken down. No treasure was found—and the column vanished, to reappear on the village green at Weybridge in Surrey. But the transmogrification was less than magical. The column had been re-erected as a memorial to the Duchess of York, who once lived in a house near Weybridge.

The Seven Dials area can be explored in many possible ways, and the following sequence indicates only one of them.

The Cambridge Theatre is one of London's newest theatres. When it opened in 1930 it was much praised for its modernity; we can now see it as a part of the much appreciated Thirties. Audrey Hepburn began a short West End career on the Cambridge stage in 1950 in a revue called *Sauce Piquant*—before she became a main dish in Hollywood.

Earlham Street has a good collection of buildings, of which Nos 4, 6, 22, 24, 26, 36, 38, 40 and 43 are listed. The Earlham Street Warehouse was once part of a mighty complex of buildings connected by iron bridges over the road; a brewery empire in which, according to a writer of 1888, even the coolers—seven of them—were 'large as fishponds, measuring 50 feet square'. Paper wholesalers, Lepard and Smiths, took over the warehouse in 1906 and when they moved away in 1972 they left behind their trademark in granite at the entrance—an L in a shield with a leopard rampant. Perhaps those noble leopards help to obliterate the lingering memory of a perfidious landlord of the public house that was apparently on the spot before the brewery. It is said that he paid off the debts of women in Newgate Debtors' Prison and, having released them from the official one, shut them up in his private prison—a nearby brothel—to work off their debt to him. This is probably true. Seven Dials was once a place where the worst that could happen usually did.

The Warehouse Donmar Theatre is at No 41, a small and excellent attachment to the Royal Shakespeare Company, whose main London activity is at the Aldwych Theatre. The facilities at the Warehouse enable them to stage quite substantial productions such as *Much Ado About Nothing* and *The Caucasian Chalk Circle.*

At No 43 there is the British Crafts Centre, which exists to promote the work of artist craftsmen, and stages exhibitions, lectures, demonstrations and discussions. Membership is open to all, but special qualifications are required from those who wish to exhibit.

Neal Street contains numerous examples of well rehabilitated 19th-century buildings. No 33 is a hallowed place where they follow the rare craft of making market barrows—together with their other establishments in Nottingham Court and Shorts Gardens. The firm of Ellen Keeley carries on unmoved by the departure of many of its natural customers in the fruit and vegetable trade, for those who need barrows will still beat a path to their door. James Keeley created the costermonger's barrow, designed for those who sold the large and once very popular costard apple; and he also had a hand in perfecting the donkey barrow—which may still have a future when the pumps run dry.

Only the frontage offers evidence of a pub, the Fountain, formerly at No 78. No 24 still has the Crown and Anchor, but the name is probably a century or more older than the present structure, which dates from 1904.

The listed buildings are many: 3-7, 17, 19, 27-37, 48, 55, 60, 61, 63, 64, 66, 68, 70, 78, 78A, 78B, 80.

Neal's Yard is especially notable for its 200-year-old armourers, Robert White & Sons. The products are for theatrical use nowadays but making them is as skilful a task as ever.

Monmouth Street recalls the Duke of Monmouth, who had a mansion over in Soho Square. The Crown public house is listed as also are Numbers 14-18, 21, 27, 29, 35, 37, 39, 49, 53-59, 61, 63-71, 73, and 75.

Listed buildings in **Tower Street** are Nos 18 North, 18 South, and 22. And in **Tower Court** they are Nos 5-8 and 10.

No 1 **West Street** is The Ivy Restaurant, an inseparable part of the theatrical world. It has long been a favourite dining place for London's actors and actresses.

The poverty common to many streets in and around Covent Garden in the 19th century is apparent in this 1876 photograph of cheap fish being sold to barefooted customers in St Giles.

No 8 is a listed building, and near to it there was formerly a chapel where John and Charles Wesley preached. No 24 is listed, and so are the Ambassadors Theatre and St Martin's Theatre. The play that opened **The Ambassadors Theatre** in 1913, *Panthea,* ran for only fifteen nights, failing by a generous margin to foreshadow the future in store for the one that had its first night there on November 25, 1952, Agatha Christie's thriller *The Mousetrap*—now in the St Martin's Theatre, next door, and due to complete its 28th year in November 1980.

The St Martin's Theatre, seating 550, was planned as a companion to the Ambassadors but arrived a little late because of the 1914-18 war, opening in the middle of it in 1916 with a comedy called *Houp La!* Its decor has been described as English Georgian. It is revered for its record-breaking *The Mousetrap,* born in the Ambassadors. See above.

Litchfield Street, though short, has four listed buildings, Nos 24 and 24A, 25, 26 and 27. Mozart is said to have lodged in the street. Thomas De Quincey lodged and starved there.

Shelton Street was named after a local benefactor who bequeathed some money in the 17th century to clothe 20 aged and educate 50 young poor people. The Covent Garden Community Centre is in the Earlham Street Warehouse on the north side. Listed buildings are Nos 1A, 1, 3, 5, 9, 11, 13, 15, 17, 19, 21, 24, 26, 34, 51, 53, 57, 59 and 61.

Mercer Street is a reminder of the Mercers' Company, long-standing landowners in Covent Garden who erected some dwellings for artisans between the wars. The Macready's Club is named after the 19th century Drury Lane actor. Nos 21 to 27 are listed.

Langley Street has a row of listed buildings, Nos 6, 7 and 8, occupying most of the northern side.

Endell Street was built in the middle of the 19th century, and one of the original buildings was the attractive Cross Keys at No 31, listed. Also listed is the elegant London Swiss Church, at No 79, erected in 1853; as well—most deservedly—as No 22 that was created for manufacturing stained-glass. A modern swimming pool, the Oasis, has very pleasantly replaced what was formerly the Bloomsbury and St Giles Baths and Wash-houses at the High Holborn end of the street. St Paul's Hospital, now a teaching hospital, has the distinction of being the oldest Lying-In Hospital in London. It began life in Betterton Street in 1749 and moved to its present site a hundred years later. Numbers 51-69, and 81 are listed buildings in addition to those already mentioned.

North-East Sector

In **Betterton Street** there is a very fine 18th century house, No 24, named Brownlow House in honour of Sir James Brownlow who had lived nearby. The street itself was called Brownlow Street up to 1877, when the honour passed to the splendid 17th century actor, Thomas Betterton. Nos 1, 24, 33 and 34 are listed buildings.

Dryden Street was only recently renamed in 1938 after the poet, also a 17th century figure.

Great Queen Street, dominated by the mammoth Freemasons' Hall, is not what it used to be. The street, named after the Queen of James I, was begun early in the 17th century and remained mainly devoted to small traders until the 19th century. The freemasons started to move in around 1776, and constant extensions culminated in the Freemasons' Hall in 1933.

The Connaught Rooms has close links with commerce and industry and is in regular use for functions and conferences. On the opposite side of the road there was once a theatre which produced the English première of Ibsen's *A Doll's House* and Synge's *Playboy of the Western World.*

Notable people who have lived and worked in Great Queen Street include Sheridan, Boswell, Thomas Arne, John Payne and the novelist Mary Russell Mitford. William Blake and Sir Joshua Reynolds both served apprenticeships there.

Listed buildings are Nos 22, 23, 27-29, 30, 31, 33-35, 36, 37, 38.

Macklin Street is named after the actor. The most interesting feature is the St Giles' Almshouses. No 17A is also listed.

Stukeley Street is named after the archaeologist Dr Stukeley, who lived nearby. It contains the City Literary Institute, which has a remarkably wide range of adult education courses. No 24 is listed.

South-East Sector

In **Drury Lane** there is a sense of great antiquity, as if a very old footpath had refused to be completely obliterated. There is some evidence, in fact, that it was a lane in the 12th century, and perhaps before that. Somewhere near the southern end there was a colony of Danes before the Conquest (of 1066)—indicated by the name Aldwych (ald-wych) meaning old colony; and Drury Lane had an earlier name, Via de Aldwych, which suggests a positive link with those riverside inhabitants of one thousand years ago.

The present name came into use after the erection of a town house, also at the southern end, by Sir William Drury in the 16th century, and Drury Lane slowly developed into a shopping and residential street. The first Sainsbury shop opened in Drury Lane in 1869, at No 173. It has also accommodated around twenty pubs in its time, but three seems to be an adequate number now. Karl Marx addressed a meeting of workers at the White Hart.

Pepys describes an immortal moment in 1667 when he was walking to Westminster. A diary entry reads 'In the way meeting many milkmaids with their garlands upon their pails, dancing with a fiddler before them; and saw pretty Nell Gwynne standing at her lodgings' door in Drury Court in her smock sleeves and bodice looking upon me; she seemed a mighty pretty creature.'

Two years earlier Pepys had recorded the first signs of the Great Plague in Drury Lane. It was on a day in June 1665 when he wrote 'This day much against my will I did in Drury Lane see two or three houses marked with a red cross upon the doors, and "Lord have mercy upon us" writ there; which was a sad sight to see, being the first of the kind that, to my remembrance, I ever saw.'

The New London Theatre, on the corner of Parker Street, is now in use for television productions. It recently replaced a theatre of great charm, the Winter Garden, which had opened in 1919 with a musical show that matched the flavour of its almost-Twenties decor, *Kissing Time.* Formerly there had been taverns on the spot since the days of the first Elizabeth, and they gradually became associated with the developing music hall tradition under the exotic name of the Mogul—after the great Mogul of Hindustan. In 1911 the premises became the New Middlesex Theatre of Varieties, but true Londoners still called it 'The Old Mo'.

Listed buildings are the Marlborough Head, No 36, and Nos 30 to 40, including the Marlborough Head, 42, 43, 44, 46 and 186-189.

Drury Lane once continued further, but the Aldwych development scheme wiped it out in 1900. The change brought into existence the Aldwych Theatre and the Strand Theatre, but it almost destroyed the old theatreland that had grown up around Drury Lane over the years. At the outset four theatres were demolished, including the Opera Comique, the Gaiety Theatre in the Strand, the Olympic Theatre in lost Wych Street, and the Globe Theatre in vanished Newcastle Street.

The Aldwych Theatre opened in 1905, and in the Twenties and Thirties it made theatrical history with the Ben Travers farces which brought together Ralph Lynn, Tom Walls, Robertson Hare and Alfred Drayton as an impeccable comedy team. Their work created a distinct category—the Aldwych farce. The theatre was threatened by further development plans in 1958 and 1959 but it was rescued by the Governors of the Shakespeare Memorial Theatre, Stratford-upon-Avon, who took it over for their London headquarters.

Catherine Street is naturally dominated by the Theatre Royal, which has its entrance in this street. It is slightly confusing, perhaps, that the theatre is still named after Drury Lane, which is at the back of it, but the apparent oddity is sanctioned by centuries of tradition, and the fact that the entrance was in Drury Lane originally.

The **Theatre Royal, Drury Lane,** that we now see is the fourth on the site. It opened in October 1812 with an address by Lord Byron. The first theatre opened in 1663 with *The Humorous Lieutenant* by Beaumont and Fletcher. It is impossible to overstate the importance of this theatre and it is dealt with more fully in earlier pages. Here we can recall that its advent released the drama from the total repression imposed by the Puritans, and that immortal Nell Gwynne rose to fame by selling a few oranges in the auditorium and then stepping on the stage to capture the hearts of London's theatregoers and Charles II.

The corner with Russell Street was once occupied by the Rose Tavern, mentioned much by Samuel Pepys and James Boswell, drawn by Hogarth, and appearing in plays by Thomas Shadwell and George Farquhar.

The Duchess Theatre, opposite, is a small theatre seating 474, which opened in 1929. It has had many successes to live down the distinction of holding a record in short runs. In 1930 *The Intimate Revue* was rung down before the end of its first night performance.

The Opera Tavern is a listed building erected in 1879 on the site of older inns. It has an attractive frontage and many theatrical souvenirs on the walls inside. The Nell of Old Drury is also a replacement of an earlier inn. Nos 15, 27 and 33 are listed.

The Strand Theatre on the Aldwych corner was originally known as the Waldorf, and opened with a season of opera and plays in 1905. Its most recent success is *No Sex Please—We're British,* which opened in June 1971 and claims to be the longest running comedy in the world.

The streets to the east of Drury Lane in this sector do not call for special attention and the visitor who is ready to see more of Covent Garden can do no better than walk back through Russell Street to the square for a final glimpse of the place where it all began.

Samuel Pepys in 1666, when he was 33.

Conservatories on the roof of the Central Market building in 1831.

Shopping in Covent Garden

Visitors and Londoners alike are discovering that Covent Garden is a very good place indeed for shopping, and it is becoming increasingly so day by day. The area attracts individualists and as a result the goods and services to be found are richly varied and, in many cases, unique.

The restored Central Market building, referred to officially as The Market, is London's first speciality late-night shopping centre, remaining open six nights a week until 8 pm. A further attraction is the number and variety of eating facilities it offers, including a coffee house, a wine bar, a wholefood bar, a pub called the Punch and Judy, a creperie, and two other restaurants. One is in a restored greenhouse that had been taken away before the turn of the century, and the other is an English style brasserie with a large all-weather sitting out area.

The tenants for the 36 units in the building were chosen with the object of providing a balanced mixture of shops that would be attractive to Londoners and visitors alike and also help to preserve the character of the area. They include shops selling British made craft goods, cosmetics, fashion and knitwear, books, gifts, confectionery, groceries, delicatessen, health foods, cheese, pottery and ceramics, household goods, herbs, tea and coffee, and toys.

There is also a firm link with the market tradition of the past in the North Hall, where forty original trading stands are available for daily or weekly lets for the sale of flowers and fruit and craft products.

The following list of shops and services in The Market is correct at the time of going to press, but changes are liable to occur at short notice.

Restaurants etc.

Mario and Franco	Restaurant
Thomas de Quincey	English style brasserie/restaurant
The Creperie	Creperie with wine licence
Danish Catering	Coffee house and patisserie with wine licence
Davy & Co	Traditional wine bar
Cranks	Vegetarian wholefood and juice bar
Courage	Punch and Judy public house

Shops

Anello and Davide	Ballet and dance clothing and footwear
The Body Shop	Natural cosmetics
Caroline Brunn	Ladies' fashion knitwear
Casa Fina	Iberian and Latin American household goods
Crockers	Crockery, pottery and china
Crocodile	Ladies' fashions
Culpeper	Herbs and spices
The Dolls House	Antique and hand-made dolls' houses, miniature furniture and accessories
Elizabeth David	Kitchen equipment and household goods
Eric Snook Toys and Models Ltd	Toys and Models
Ferns	Tea and coffee provisions and accessories
Fiorucci	Ladies' fashions
Hammick's	Bookshop
Inside Out Shop/Covent Garden Central Store	General gift merchandise and 'Covent Garden' products
Kickers	Adults' and children's footwear and accessories
Monsoon	Ladies' and children's clothing
National Dairy Council	English cheese and dairy products
Naturally British	British made craft goods, pottery, toys, knitwear and fabrics
Original and Rare Newspaper Company	Rare newspapers and periodicals
Pamela Price	Groceries and delicatessen
Penguins	Paperback books
Rural Crafts Association	British craft merchandise in natural materials
Strangeways	Pottery, ceramics and associated goods
Thornton's	Chocolates and other confectionery

The streets leading to the Piazza, and the traditional local shopping street, Drury Lane, are also being revitalised. But little shops and small hives of industry are everywhere, and many of the most interesting are only to be discovered by wandering among the narrow streets that meander in all directions. One should not overlook the old thoroughfare of Long Acre, with major establishments such as the Arts Council shop, Stanford's, Harveys Auction Rooms and Paxman of Covent Garden, bright with brass instruments.

Marketing and craft activities worthy of special attention take place under and around The Jubilee Market. It has an antique market on Mondays and a collector's market on Tuesdays. On Saturdays the spot becomes London's biggest craft market, looked after by the London Craft Centre. The stallholders are enthusiastic, and many of them give demonstrations of pottery-making, wood-turning, cotton-spinning and other crafts. The future of this activity is uncertain, however, as the Jubilee Hall may not survive after 1982, when perhaps an alternative site may be found.

Mrs Patrick Campbell buying flowers from Polly Pegg, the flower girl, in 1920.

Guide to Shops and Services

The following lists are offered as a general guide only and do not aim to be complete. Omissions do not in any way imply adverse criticism. Every effort has been made to provide information that is correct at the time of going to press, but accuracy cannot be entirely guaranteed as changes can occur at short notice. The map references give the location of the street in which the premises are situated, but not necessarily the premises themselves.

Art Galleries, Antiques and Auction Rooms

Acme Gallery	43 Shelton St	121 C5
Anthony Stokes	3 Langley Ct	125 D6
	Gallery and bookshop	
Anthropos Gallery	65-67 Monmouth St	121 B5
Arthur Middleton	12 New Row	124 C8
	Pre-1880 scientific instruments	
British Crafts Centre	43 Earlham St	121 B5
	Craft gallery and shop	
Cathay Antiques	47 Monmouth St	121 B5
	Chinese and Japanese antiques	
Covent Garden Gallery	20 Russell St	125 F6
Dryden Street Gallery	5 Dryden St	122 E4
Edward Totah Gallery	39 Floral St	125 D6
Harvey's Auction Rooms	22-23 Long Acre	122 D5
	Antiques, rare books, etc	
Hester van Royan Gallery	1 Langley Ct	125 D6
	Contemporary art	
Japanese Gallery	47 Bedford St	125 D8
Neal Street Gallery	56 Neal St	121 C4
The Old Drury	187 Drury Lane	122 E3
	Antiques	
Photographers Gallery	8 Great Newport St	124 B7
	Photographic exhibitions	
Sandford Gallery	1 Mercer St	121 B5

Banks and Post Offices

Barclays	5 Henrietta St	125 D8
Lloyds	22 Southampton St	125 F8
	and 83 Long Acre	125 D5
Midland	70 St Martin's Lane	124 B8

Nat-West	34 Henrietta St	125 D8
	and 1 Long Acre	125 D5
Post Offices	24 William IV St	124 C9
	and 3 Southampton St	125 F8

Books, Maps and Magazines

Alternative Bookshop	40 Floral St Libertarian book specialist	125 D6
Arts Council Shop	8 Long Acre Art exhibition catalogues, posters, reproductions, postcards, slides replicas, books. Also poetry readings, talks and exhibitions	122 D5
Bell, Book & Radmall	80 Long Acre First editions, biography, science fiction	122 D5
Booksmith	33 Maiden Lane	125 E8
Corner House Bookshop	14 Endell St Radical books and magazines	121 C3
J. B. Cramer & Co	99 St Martin's Lane Sheet music, books, recorders	124 B8
Dorling Kindersley	9 Henrietta St Publishers and general booksellers	125 D8
Samuel French	26 Southampton St Plays, books on theatre, sound effects and dialect recordings	125 F8
Hammicks	The Market Wide range of books	125 E7
Jarndyce	68 Neal St Antiquarian books	121 C4
Lake & Brooks	106 Bedford Chambers Philatelic books, stamps, postcards	125 D8
Mapsellers	37 Southampton St Antique maps, atlases, globes	125 F8
Bertram Rota	30-31 Long Acre Antique books	122 D5
Ian Shipley Books	34 Floral St Books on the arts	125 D6
Penguins	The Market Paperback books	125 E7
Specatator Publications	91 St. Martin's Lane Books on advertising, public relations and publishing	124 B8
Original and Rare Newspaper Co	The Market Rare newspapers and periodicals	125 E7

Edward Stanford	12-14 Long Acre Map Specialists Maps and guidebooks of anywhere in the world. Charts, globes, atlases; books on architecture/enviroment; selected paperbacks	124 C6
Bernard Stone	43 Floral St Poetry, modern first editions, small presses, illustrated and secondhand books, children's books, poetry broadsheets, Turret books, Benn Graphics	125 D6
Vintage Magazine Shop	2-4 Earlham St Old magazines	121 B5

Clothes and Shoes

Anello & Davide	The Market, and 30 Drury Lane Dance clothing and shoes	125 E7 122 E3
Caroline Brunn	The Market Ladies' fashion knitwear	125 E7
Chris Trill	17 Catherine St Fashion accessories	126 G6
Clive Shilton	58 Neal St Shoes, handbags, belts etc	121 C4
Crocodile	The Market Ladies' fashions	125 E7
Fig Leaf	3 Russell St Ladies' fashions	125 F6
Fiorucci	The Market Ladies' fashions	125 E7
S. Fisher	20-22 Wellington St Scottish knitwear	126 G7
Galicia	24 Wellington St Clothes for women	126 G7
Howie	138 Long Acre Design and fashion shop	122 D5
Kickers	The Market Adults' and children's footwear	125 E7
Laines Anny Blatt	20 Bedford St Knitting wool, patterns, designs	125 D8
Laura Ashley	35 Bow St. Garments and home furnishings	122 E5
Les 2 Zebres	34 & 38 Tavistock St Fashions for men and women	125 F7
Lloyde Jennings	54-56 Neal St Shoes	121 C4
Made in Heaven	18-19 Long Acre Jeans, pants and other clothes	122 D5

Mayfair	60 Neal St Fashions and men's wear	121 C4
Metropolis	63 Shelton St Men's and women's collections	121 C5
Miss Edwina	160 Drury Lane Ladies' fashion shoes	122 E3
Monsoon	The Market Ladies' and children's clothing	125 E7
Moss Bros	Bedford St Formal clothes for hire. Also general sales with fashions for younger men a speciality	125 D8
Natural Shoe Store	21 Neal St	121 C4
No. 16	16 Russell St Fashion designers' collections	125 F6
C. Porselli	9 West St Ballet wear	121 A5
Paul Smith	44 Floral St Men's fashions	125 D6
Pygmalion	15 Drury Lane Ladies' fashions	122 E3
Scottish Merchant	16 New Row Knitwear	124 C8
Succhi	40 Wellington St Shoes and clothing	126 G7
Tuareg	169 Drury Lane Ladies' clothes and accessories	122 E3
Ulla Ward	26 Wellington St Knitwear	126 G7

An early example of advertising by a Piazza dressmaker.

Crafts, Household Goods, Gifts, Toys etc

Africa Centre	38 King St Handicrafts from developing countries	125 D7
Aram Designs	3 Kean St Modern furniture and light fittings	123 H4
The Bath and Bed Shop	2 Russell St Bathroom and bedroom accessories	125 F6
The Beadshop	39 Neal St Beads	121 C4
British Crafts Centre	43 Earlham St Craft gallery and shop	121 B5
Casa Fina	The Market Iberian and Latin American household goods	125 E7
Catz	25 Bedfordbury Books, prints and gifts featuring cats	124 C8
Co-Existence	2 Conduit Ct Modern furnishings and design	124 C6
Covent Garden Workshop	1 Banbury Ct Handmade pine furniture	125 D6
Crockers	The Market Crockery, pottery and china	125 E7
The Dolls House	The Market Antique and hand-made dolls' houses and furniture	125 E7
Elizabeth David	The Market Kitchen equipment, household goods	125 E7
Frida	111 Long Acre Third world handicrafts	122 D5
Glasshouse	65 Long Acre Glassblowing workshop and gallery	122 D5
Harvest	40 Tavistock St British crafts	
The Inside Out Shop	The Market, and 107 Long Acre General store	125 F7 122 D5
The Kite Store	69 Neal St Kites	121 C4
Knutz	1 Russell St Modern and antique toys	125 F6
The Lampshop	24 Bedfordbury Lamps and lighting	124 C8
Naturally British	The Market and 13 New Row British-made craft goods, pottery, toys, knitwear and fabrics	125 F7 124 C8

The Neal Street Shop	29 Neal St Gifts, cards, toys	121 C4
The New Neal Street Shop	23 Neal St Gifts featuring plants & flowers, Chinese jewellery, antiques, embroideries	121 C4
Paper Rainbow	17 Monmouth St Cards and gifts	121 B5
Paul Wu	64 Long Acre Oriental handicrafts	122 D5
The Pine Shop	32 Shelton St	121 C5
Rural Crafts Association	The Market British craftwork in natural materials	125 E7
Eric Snook	The Market Toys and models	125 E7
Strangeways	The Market Pottery, ceramics etc.	125 E7

Food

Augustus Barnett	36 Wellington St Wines and spirits	126 G7
Robert Bruce	19 James St Fruit and vegetables	122 D5
Cheong-Leen	4-10 Tower St Chinese Supermarket	121 B5
Civil Service Stores	425 Strand Department store	125 E9
Culpeper	The Market Herbs and spices	125 E7
Drury Lane Tea & Coffee Co	37 Drury Lane and 3 New Row Tea and coffee	122 E3 124 C8
Fern's	The Market Tea and coffee	125 E7
The Golden Orient	17 Earlham St Wholefood and spices	121 B5
Hobbs	3 Garrick St Provisions and delicatessen	124 C7
National Dairy Council	The Market English cheese, dairy produce	125 E7
Neal's Yard Bakery	6 Neal's Yard Bakery	121 C4
Neal's Yard Dairy	9 Neal's Yard Dairy produce	121 C4
Neal's Yard Wholefood Warehouse	2 Neal's Yard Wholefoods in bulk packs	121 C4
Oddbins	23 Earlham St Wines and spirits	121 B5
Old Chelsea Wine Stores	11 Russell St Wine shippers	125 F6

Robert Portwine	24 Earlham St Butcher	121 B5
Pamela Price	The Market Groceries and delicatessen	125 E7
Scott's Delicatessen	6 Shorts Gardens	121 C4
Shepherd Foods (London)	24 Drury Lane Supermarket	122 E3
Thornton's	The Market Chocolates/confectionery	125 E7

Libraries

High Holborn Library	198 High Holborn	122 D2
Westminster Library	4 Charing Cross Road	124 A7
Westminster Central Reference Library	St. Martin's St	124 A7
British Library	9-13 Kean St Science Reference Library Annexe	123 H4

Miscellaneous Shops and Organizations

Alberts	1 Betterton Street Florists	122 D3
The Badge Shop	18 Earlham St Slogan and picture badges	121 B5
Arthur Beale	194 Shaftsbury Ave Yacht chandlers; rope	121 B3
Thos Bland & Sons	21 New Row Rifles; shotguns	124 C8
The Body Shop	The Market Natural cosmetics	125 E7
Coppershop	48 Neal St English-made copperware	121 C4
Covent Garden Cycles	41 Shorts Gardens New and secondhand bicycles	121 C4
Covent Garden Sports	17 Maiden Lane Supplies for sport	125 E8
Dance Centre	11-14 Floral St Lessons and exercises, solarium, spa, sauna, swimming pool. Leisurewear shops at	125 D6
	22 Wellington St	126 G7
	and 20 Cecil Ct.	124 B8
Detail	49 Endell St Modern jewellery, accessories	121 C3
Charles H Fox	25 Shelton St Theatre costumes and make-up	121 C5
Ellen Keeley	33 Neal St Makers of market barrows	121 C4
Ellen Keeley	4 Shorts Gdns Florists	121 C4

The Kite Shop	69 Neal St
Kites	121 C4
C & W May	9 Garrick St
Theatrical costumiers	124 C7
Moss Bros	Bedford St
Formal dress hire. Sales also.	125 D8
Parker's of London	12 Upper St Martin's Lane
Supplies for horses, riding, polo	124 B6
Studio 51	10-11 Great Newport St
Classical and contemporary
dance classes	124 B7
Penhaligons	41 Wellington St
Perfumiers	126 G7
Royal Opera House	48 Floral St
Box Office and information	125 D6
J. Roberts & Sons	5 King St
Rifles and shotguns	125 D7
Robert White & Sons	25 Shelton St
Theatrical armourers and
jewellers	121 C5
Shylocks	10 Russell St
Hair designers	125 F6
Studio Gallery	8 Garrick St
Silver and jewellery	124 C7
Suttons Seeds	33 Catherine St
Flower and vegetable seeds	
Theatre Zoo	28 New Row
and 21 Earlham St
Animal costumes for hire.
Masks, make-up etc.	124 C8
121 B5
Walter Davies	40 St. Martin's Lane
Jewellery and silverware	124 B8
Youth Hostel Assocn.	14 Southampton St
Camping, sports and leisure-wear	125 F8

Music, Instruments and Records

Breitkopf & Hartel	20 Earlham St
Music publishers	121 B5
Covent Garden Records	20 James St
Records and cassettes	122 D5
Honest Jons Records	9 Monmouth St	121 B5
James Asman	23A New Row
Records	124 C8
Paxman of Covent Garden	116 Long Acre
Makers of French horns;
suppliers and repairers of
brass instruments	122 D5
Phoenix Music Co	49 Neal St
Records and cassettes	121 C4
Raymond Man Chinese
Music Shop	6 Earlham St	121 B5

Rock Dreams	44 Wellington St	126 G7
	Records and cassettes	
Salvi Harps	55 Endell St	121 C3
	Harp makers	

Philately

Harris Publications	42 Maiden Lane	125 E8
	Stamp accessories	
Lake & Brooks	106 Bedford Chambers	124 C8
	Stamps, albums, philatelic books	
London Stamp Centre	27 Maiden Lane	125 E8
	Stamp dealers	
Royale Stamp Co	41-42 Bedford St	125 D8
	Stamp dealers	
Stanley Gibbons	Drury House, Russell St	125 F6
	Also at 391, 395 and 399	125 E9
	Strand and at 37 Southampton St	125 F8
	Stamps, auctioneers	

Covent Garden Administration

Covent Garden Community Association	43-45 Shorts Gardens	121 C4
	Support for more housing and community life	
Covent Garden Forum	205 Bedford Chambers	124 C8
	Elected representatives of public opinion in Covent Garden, advising and consulted by GLC	
Covent Garden Enterprise	5 Dryden St	122 E4
	Help for small businesses	
Covent Garden Association	28/29 Southampton St	125 F8
	Local traders' organisation. Publishes *Covent Garden Advertiser*	
GLC Covent Garden Team	1 King St	125 D7
	Planning team for Covent Garden development	

Churches

Corpus Christi Church (RC)	Maiden Lane	125 E8
St Martin-in-the-Field (C of E)	St Martin's Place	124 B10
St Paul's Church (C of E)	Inigo Place	125 D7
Scottish National Church	Crown Court	122 F5
Swiss Church	Endell St	121 C3

Theatres, Restaurants and Hotels

Many visitors to London have already discovered that there is much to be gained by staying at a hotel in or on the fringe of Covent Garden. It is obviously well placed for visiting the Royal Opera House and the other theatres that abound in the area, and it has good places for eating out. It can be a pleasant change to walk back to base after an evening out instead of bothering about transport. Covent Garden is also well situated for visiting the National Gallery, the British Museum, Whitehall, Westminster, Buckingham Palace, Somerset House, and the concert halls and theatres on the South Bank. Above all, perhaps, Covent Garden has a homely atmosphere, and the odd few minutes can always be spent enjoyably in getting to know it better.

Theatres

Box office phone numbers are shown. See daily press for performance details

Adelphi	Strand Tel. 836 7611	125 E9
Albery	St Martin's Lane Tel. 836 3878	124 B8
Aldwych	Aldwych Tel. 836 6404 Royal Shakespeare Company	126 H6
Ambassadors	West St Tel. 836 1171	121 A5
Arts	Gt Newport St Tel. 836 3334 Includes Unicorn Theatre for Young People	124 B7
Cambridge	Earlham St Tel. 836 6056	121 B5
Coliseum	St Martin's Lane Tel. 836 3161 English National Opera and visiting companies	124 B8
Drury Lane (Theatre Royal)	Catherine St Tel. 836 8108	126 G6
Duchess	Catherine St Tel. 836 8243	126 G6
Duke of Yorks	St Martin's Lane Tel. 836 5122	124 B8
Fortune	Russell St Tel. 836 2238	123 G5
Garrick	Charing Cross Road Tel. 836 4601	124 A7
New London	Drury Lane Tel. 405 0072 In use as TV studio	126 G6
Royal Opera House	Bow St Tel. 240 1066 Royal Opera and Royal Ballet	122 E5
St Martin's	West St Tel. 836 1443	121 A5
Strand	Aldwych Tel. 836 2660	126 H6
Vaudeville	Strand Tel. 836 9988	125 E9

Warehouse (Donmar Theatre)	Earlham St Tel. 836 6808 Small productions by Royal Shakespeare Company	121 B5
Wyndham's	Charing Cross Rd Tel. 836 3028	124 A7

Hotels

Charing Cross	Strand Tel. 839 7282	125 E9
Drury Lane	Drury Lane Tel. 836 6666	122 E3
Fielding	4 Broad Court Tel. 836 8305	122 E4
Pastoria	St. Martin's St Tel. 930 8641	124 A7
Savoy	Strand Tel. 836 4343	125 E9
Shaftesbury	Monmouth St Tel. 836 4422	121 B5
Strand Palace	Strand Tel. 836 8080	125 E9
Waldorf	Aldwych Tel. 836 2400	126 H6

Restaurants

Ajimura Japanese Restaurant	51-53 Shelton Street Tel. 240 0178	121 C5
Beotys	79 St Martin's Lane Tel. 836 8768	124 B6
Blitz	4 Gt Queen St Tel. 405 6598 Winebar, restaurant	122 F3
Boulestin	25 Southampton Street Tel. 836 7061	125 F8
Chez Solange	11 St Martin's Ct and 35 Cranbourn St Tel. 836 0542	124 A7
Cranks	The Market	125 E7
Creperie	The Market	125 E7
Danish Catering	The Market	125 E7
Davy & Co	The Market	125 E7
Food for Thought	31 Neal St Tel. 836 0239	121 C4
Friends	30 Wellington St Tel. 836 5620	126 G7
The Grange	39 King St Tel. 240 2939	125 D7
Grunts' Chicago Pizza Co	12 Maiden Lane Tel. 379 7722	125 E8
Inigo Jones	14 Garrick St Tel. 836 6456	124 C7
Ivy	1 West St Tel. 836 4751	121 A5
Joe Allen	13 Exeter St Tel. 836 0651	125 F7
La Scala	35 Southampton St Tel. 240 1030	125 F8
L'Opera	31 Great Queen St Tel. 405 9020	122 F3
Luigi's	15 Tavistock St Tel. 240 1795	125 F7
Mario and Franco	The Market	125 E7
Neal Street	26 Neal St Tel. 836 8368	121 C4
Paulos'	28 Wellington St Tel. 240 1919	126 G7
Punch and Judy	The Market	125 E7
Poons of Covent Garden	41 King St Tel. 240 1743	125 D7

Porters	17 Henrietta St Tel. 836 6466	125 D8
Rock Garden	6 The Piazza Tel. 240 3961	125 E6
Rules	35 Maiden Lane Tel. 836 5314	125 E8
Rumours	33 Wellington Street Tel. 836 0038	126 G7
Thomas de Quincey's	The Market, and	125 E7
	36 Tavistock St Tel. 240 3972	125 F7
Tuttons	11 Russell St Tel. 836 1167	125 F6

Public Houses

Angel & Crown	St Martin's Lane	124 B8
Avenue Bar	Shaftesbury Avenue	121 B3
Bedford Head	Maiden Lane	125 E8
Black Horse	St Martin's Lane	124 B8
Bodega	Bedford St	125 D8
Chandos	St Martin's Lane	124 B8
Cross Keys	Endell St	121 C3
Crown	Seven Dials	121 B5
Freemason's Arms	Long Acre	122 D5
Frigate	Upper St Martin's Lane	124 B6
Green Man & French Horn	St Martin's Lane	124 B8
Kemble's Head	Long Acre/Bow St	122 E5
King's Arms	Long Acre/Langley Ct	125 D6
Lamb & Flag	Rose St	124 C7
Lemon Tree	Bedfordbury	124 C8
Lyceum Tavern	Strand	125 E9
Market House	Russell St	125 F6
Marlborough Head	Drury Lane	122 E3
Marquess of Anglesey	Russell St/Bow St	125 F6
Marquis of Granby	Shaftesbury Avenue	121 B3
Nags Head	James St/Floral St	122 D5
Nell Gwynne Tavern	Bull Inn Court	125 E8
Nell of Old Drury	Catherine St	126 G6
Old Bell	Exeter St	125 F7
Opera Tavern	Catherine St	126 G6
Peacock	Maiden Lane	125 E8
Porcupine	Charing Cross Road	124 A7
Prince of Wales	Drury Lane/Gt Queen St	122 E3
Round House	New Row/Garrick St	124 C8
Salisbury	St Martin's Lane	124 B8
Sugar Loaf	Gt Queen St	122 F3
Sun	Drury Lane	122 E3
Sun Tavern	Long Acre	122 D5
Sussex	Long Acre/Upper St Martin's Lane	124 B6
Two Brewers	Monmouth St	121 B5
Welsh Harp	Chandos Place	124 C9
White Hart	Drury Lane	122 E3
White Lion	James St/Floral St	125 D6
White Swan	New Row	124 C8

Index of Streets and Landmarks

The map references in this list give the number of the page followed by the grid reference. The text references are intended for use in locating the page on which there is a description of the features of interest in the street.

Street	Map reference	Text reference
Adelaide Street	124 C10	92
Agar Street	125 D9	92
Aldwych	126 H6	
Arne Street	122 E3	
Banbury Court	125 D6	
Bedford Court	124 C8	
Bedford Street	125 D8	84
Bedfordbury	124 C8	94
Betterton Street	122 D3	98
Bow Street	122 E5	87
Bow Street Police Station	122 F5	88
Broad Court	122 E4	90
Brydges Place	124 C9	
Bull Inn Court	125 E8	82
Burleigh Street	126 G7	87
Car Park (Bedfordbury)	124 C8	
Car Park (Drury Lane)	122 E3	
Catherine Street	126 G6	100
Cecil Court	124 B8	92
Covent Garden	125 E6	
Covent Garden Underground	122 D5	
Chandos Place	124 C9	92
Charing Cross Road	124 A7	94
Conduit Court	124 C6	
Cranbourn Street	124 B7	94
Crown Court	122 F5	
Dragon Yard	122 E1	
Drury Lane	122 E3	99
Dryden Street	122 E4	99
Earlham Street	121 B5	95
Endell Street	121 C3	98

Street	Map reference	Text reference
Exchange Court	125 E8	82
Exeter Street	125 F7	86
Floral Hall	122 F5	87
Floral Street	125 D6	74
Flower Market Building	126 G6	77
Garrick Street	124 C7	75
Goodwin's Court	124 C8	92
Great Newport Street	124 B7	94
Great Queen Street	122 F3	99
Hanover Place	122 E5	
Heathcock Court	125 E9	
Henrietta Street	125 D8	81
Hop Gardens	124 C8	94
High Holborn	122 D2	
Inigo Place	125 D7	
James Street	122 D5	74
Jubilee Hall and Market	125 F7	77
Kean Street	123 H4	
Keeley Street	123 G3	
Kemble Street	123 G4	
King Street	125 D7	75
Kingsway	123 H3	
Langley Court	125 D6	
Langley Street	121 C5	98
Leicester Square Underground	124 A7	
Litchfield Street	124 A6	98
Long Acre	122 D5	90
Lumley Court	125 E8	82
Macklin Street	122 E2	99
Maiden Lane	125 E8	82
Market, The	125 E7	77
Martlett Court	122 F5	
Mathews Yard	121 C3	
Mays Buildings	124 C8	
Mercer Street	121 B5	98
Monmouth Street	121 B5	96
National Gallery	124 A10	94
National Portrait Gallery	124 A9	94
National Theatre Museum (planned)	126 G6	77
Neal Street	121 C4	96
Neals Yard	121 C4	96
New Row	124 C8	94
Newton Street	122 F1	
Nottingham Court	121 C4	

Street	Map reference	Text reference
Old Brewers' Yard	121 C5	
The Piazza	125 E6	78
Parker Street	122 F2	
Rose Street	124 C7	74
Royal Opera House	122 E5	87
Russell Street	125 F6	78
St Giles in the Fields Church	121 A3	91
St Martin in the Fields Church	124 B10	91
St Martin's Court	124 A7	
St Martin's Lane	124 B8	90
St Paul's Church	125 E6	77
Seven Dials	121 B5	95
Shaftesbury Avenue	121 B3	
Shelton Street	121 C5	98
Shorts Gardens	121 C4	
Slingsby Place	124 C6	
Smarts Place	122 E2	
Southampton Street	125 F8	84
Strand	125 E9	92
Stukeley Street	122 E2	99
Tavistock Street	125 F7	84
Theatre Royal	123 G5	100
Tower Court	121 B5	96
Tower Street	121 B5	96
Transport Museum	126 G6	77
Upper Saint Martin's Lane	124 B6	
Wellington Street	126 G7	87
West Street	121 A5	96
Wild Court	123 G3	
Wild Street	122 F3	
William IV Street	124 C9	92

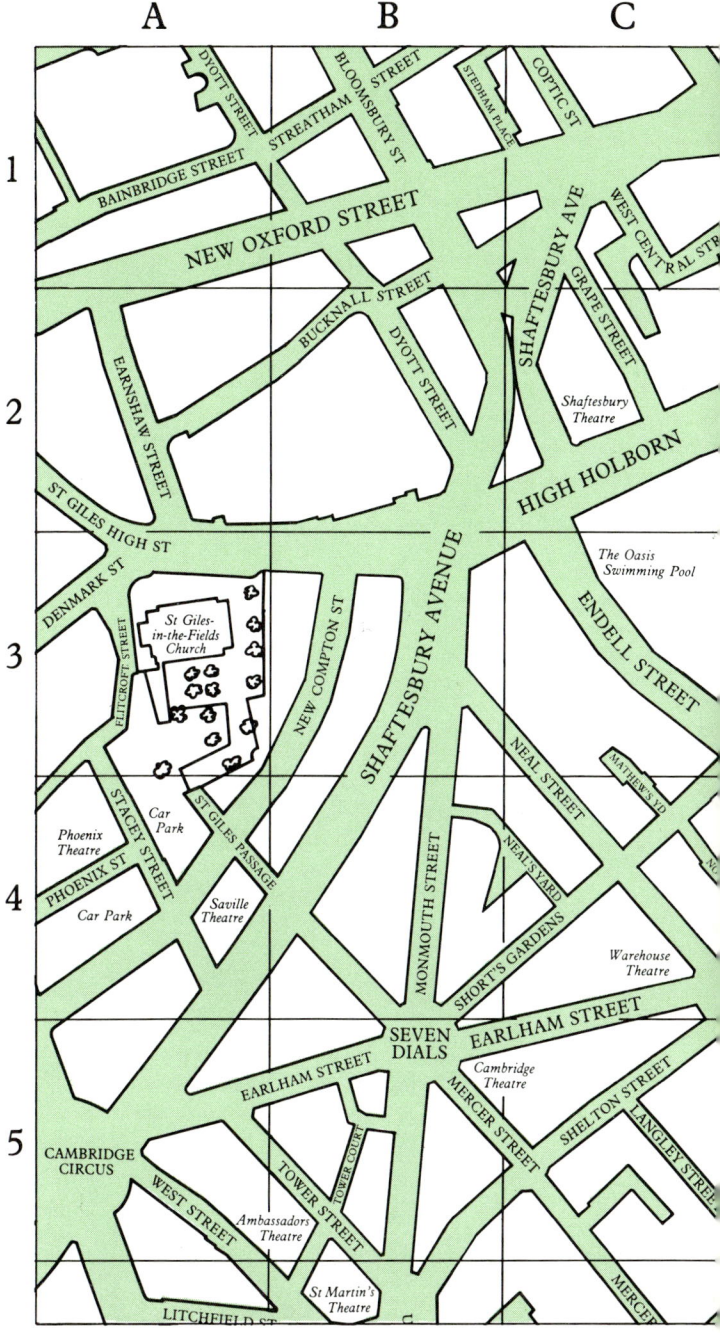

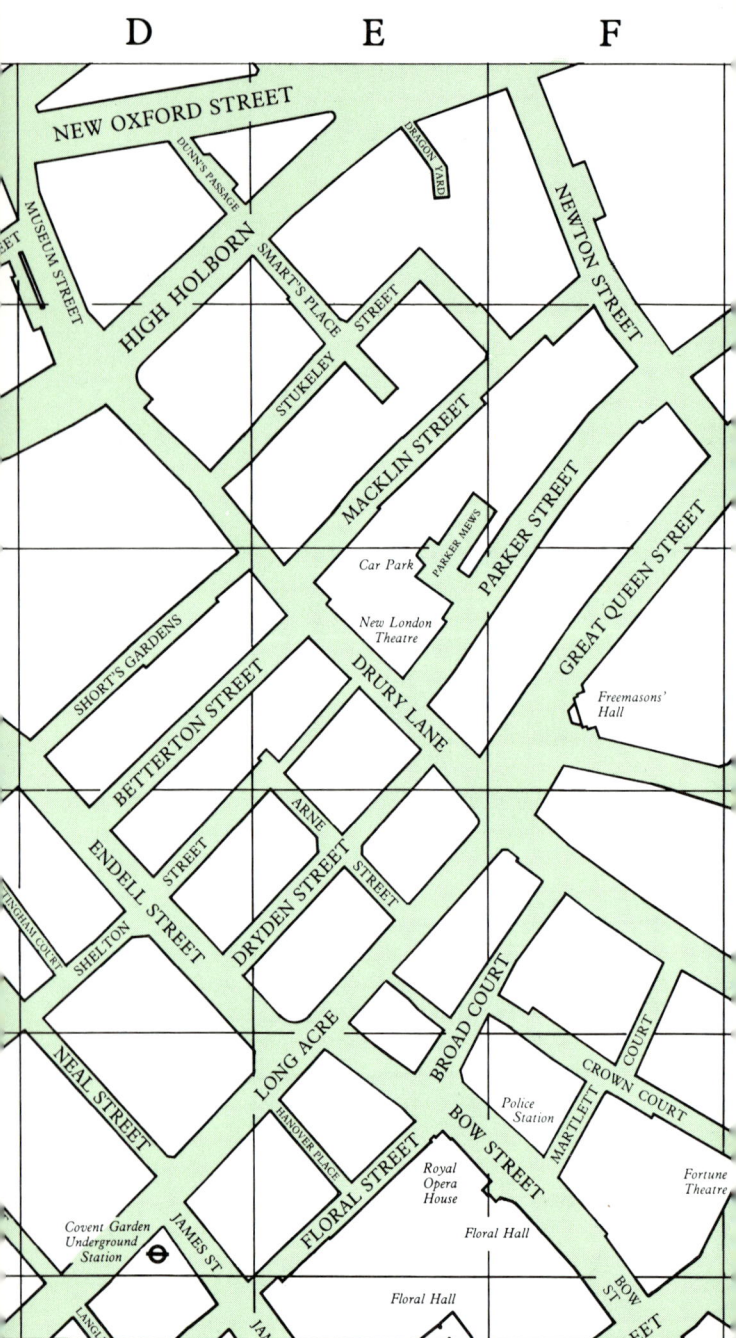

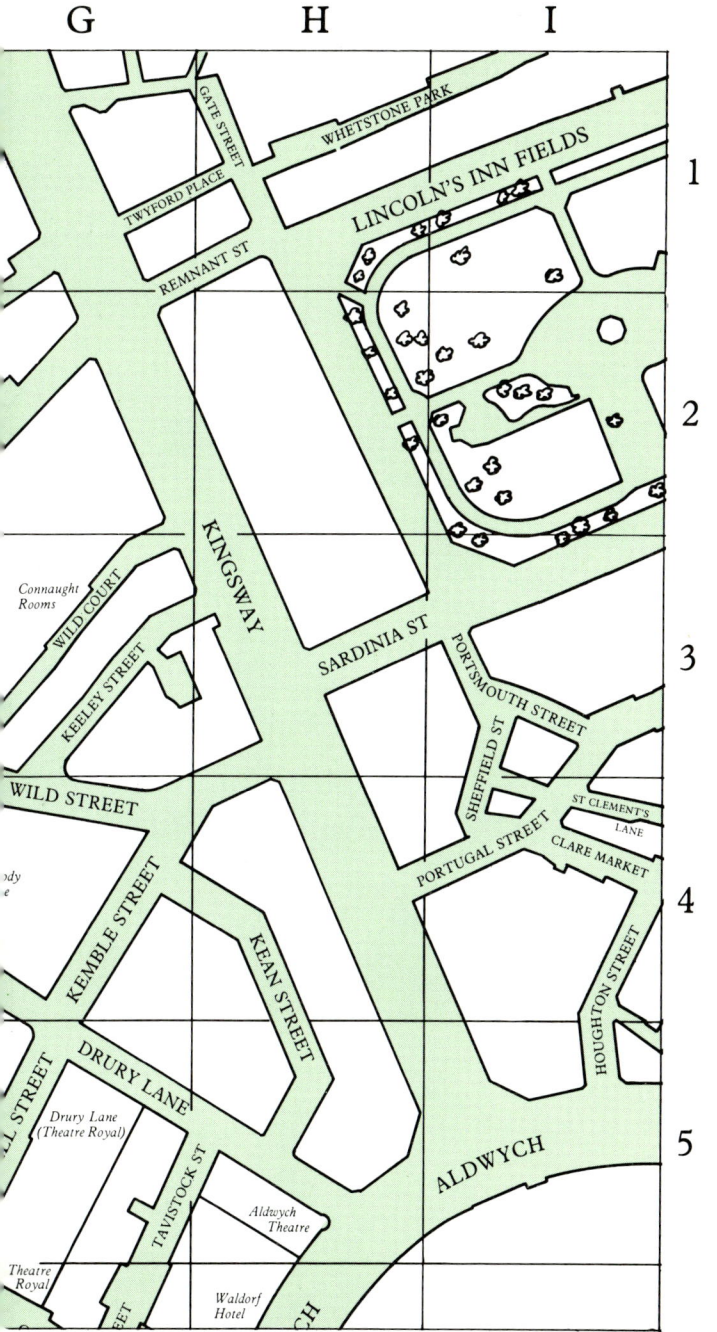

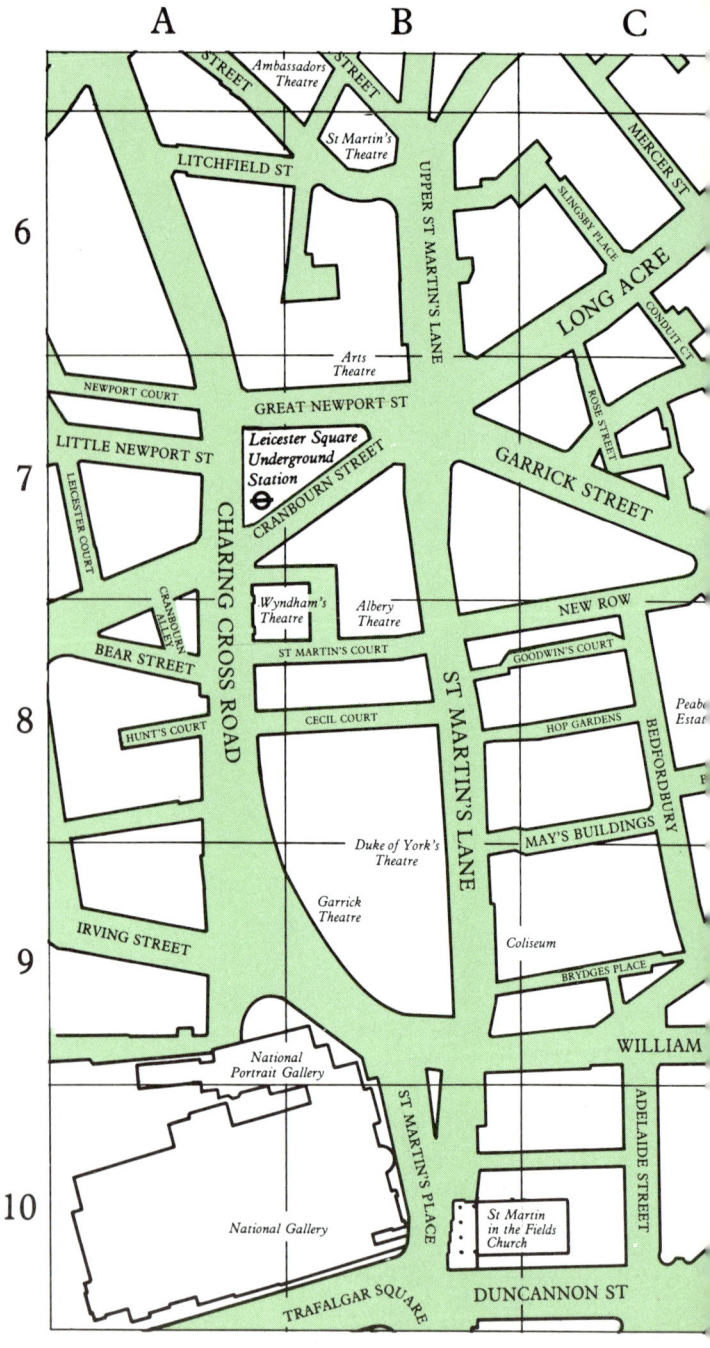

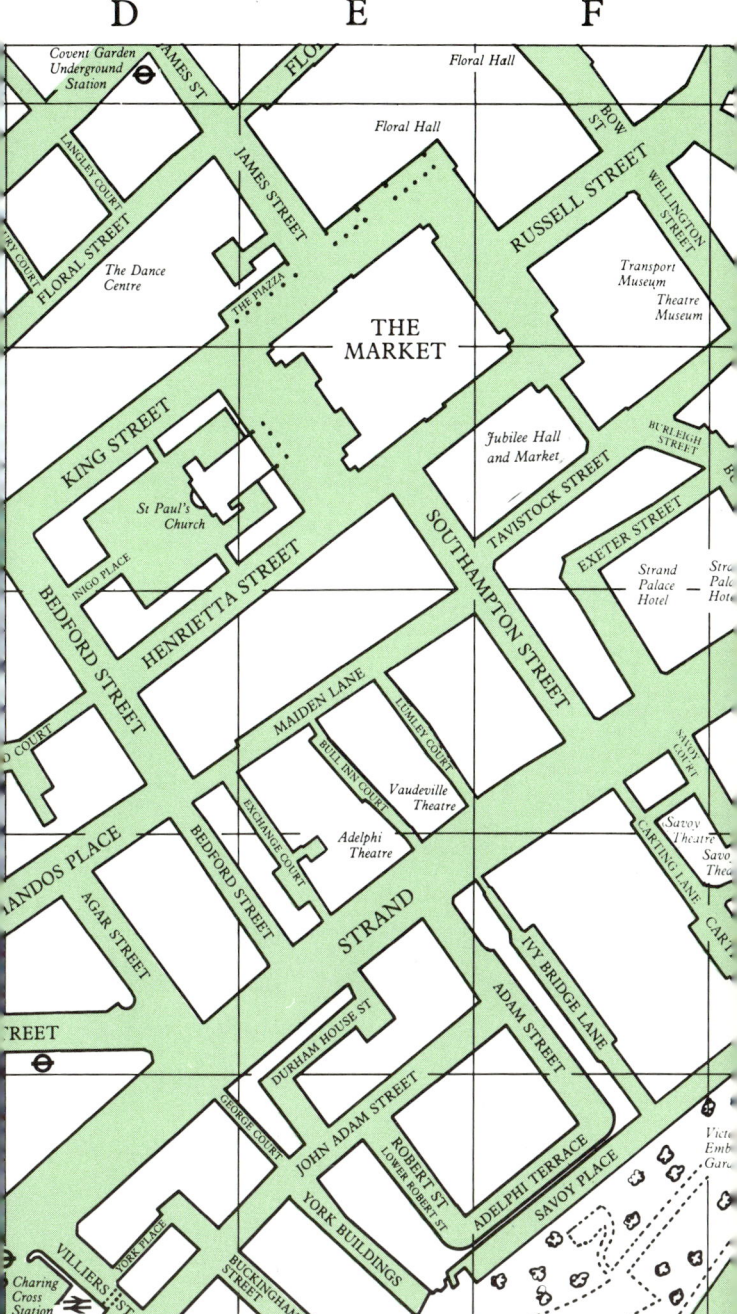